LEAVING
THE
AMISH

TO SERVE WITH HONOR

SIMON S. TROYER

MINDSTIR MEDIA

STACEY SNYDER'S
studio

3048 Cocolamus creek Rd.
Thompsontown PA 17094
Phone: 717 602 6190
www.staceysnyderstudio.com

Cover Photo, by, Stacey Snyder

Published by Mindstir Media, LLC
45 Lafayette Rd | Suite 181| North Hampton, NH 03862 | USA
1.800.767.0531 | www.mindstirmedia.com

Printed in the United States of America
ISBN-13: 978-1-958729-68-7 (Paperback)

For he is God's minister to you for good,
But if you do evil, be afraid for he does not
Bear the sword in vain for he is God's minister,
An avenger to execute wrath on him who
Practices evil.

Rom. 13, 4

DEDICATION

I dedicate this book to my wife Denise, who has stood by me all these years.
And to my father, Sam M. Troyer, who never faltered in his love for me.
And to my mother, Lizzy Troyer, whom I never met.

CONTENTS

NOTE FROM THE AUTHOR

LEAVING THE AMISH TO SERVE WITH HONOR is my story of what it was like growing up Amish and eventually breaking away to chase a dream. I was met with challenges that, at times, seemed insurmountable, along with setbacks and failures. There was a steep price to pay for my choice to leave the Amish church. I am still shunned by the church and family members, who are still Amish.

When I decided to sit down and write about my life, I didn't realize how difficult it would be. Some parts made me laugh out loud, other parts caused so many tears to flow that I had to stop writing for a while. There were a few places where it was utterly heart wrenching and almost impossible to write about. Somehow, with God's Grace, I was able to continue writing to completion.

I have known so many young people that also made their escape from the confines of the Amish, but, with seemingly no plans for the future. This often ended badly for them; often they would struggle along for a few years, then ultimately return home in failure. Others continued to struggle along without furthering their education, thus ending up with dead-end jobs, barely able to exist. Others, who had a plan and tried to stick to it, were able, with time, to reach a place in their life where they were comfortable. Some flourished. My advice to anyone planning to leave is, have a plan or two, and should you fail, get up, dust yourself off, and try again. Don't blame your failures on your past. By having a sense of pride in the way you were raised, you can use that experience to your advantage. Good luck.

Most members of the Armed Forces, have, and will continue, to serve their country with HONOR. Far too many have suffered, and many have paid the ultimate price in honorable service. I salute them. The title to my book, in no way, is meant to diminish their honorable service. Instead, it is meant to reflect the way I tried to serve, with pride and honor. I sincerely hope, you the reader, find this book interesting, if not inspirational.

This is the story of my life.

CHAPTER

1

In the Beginning

It was a cold winter evening around six pm when my mother told Dad it was time, so Dad sent all but the oldest girls to bed. He then closed the bedroom door, and Dad delivered me without a doctor present. Afterwards he gathered the family and announced my arrival. There wasn't much fanfare as is somewhat normal when you're the eleventh child. Oh sure, there was the usual everyone taking turns to hold me but I assume that excitement soon waned when the first diaper needed to be changed, and thus began my life on this earth, born into an old order Amish family. Little did I know the many challenges and hardships I would face in the future along with the many blessings bestowed on me by the Lord God.

Dad and mom lived in Berne co., Indiana during the late 1940'. They were members of a very strict old order Amish Church. I don't know much about that time except our family never had much money. In fact, we barely squeaked by most of the time. Dad wasn't much of a businessman; mostly he did odd carpenter jobs and operated a small farm where he raised enough produce to feed the family and enough hay to feed a few goats, sheep, and a mismatched team of horses. Dad and Mom were deeply religious and lived their lives accordingly. One of Dad's biggest concerns was never to overcharge anyone that he worked for, or to take advantage of anyone, and to my knowledge, he never took a government handout of any kind.

Mid 1940s, Dad and Mom decided Tennessee would be a better place to make a living, probably because of cheaper land prices, so he and mom packed up the little ones and moved to Hohenwald Tenn. where Dad tried his hand at, you guessed it, odd carpenter jobs and this time farming hard red clay, so well-known in the south that over time he was able to grow a little corn. He also purchased some chickens with the intentions of selling eggs for a little cash income, so, while waiting for the chickens to lay eggs, they still needed the usual staples, flour, yeast, and so forth, and not having any cash Dad began a small credit at the local grocery store, which in time grew to a whopping eighty dollars. At this time Dad decided he'd had enough. The chickens refused to lay eggs, and he felt there wasn't anything to gain by keeping them, so he told Mom, "We're going to sell the chickens and eat the corn ourselves," and according to what he told me, that is exactly what they did. One crop that did quite well was sweet potatoes, so from that moment on it was corn mush and sweet potatoes, fried mush and sweet potatoes, hominy and sweet potatoes, you get the picture. There was still the credit at the store that needed to be taken care of, so Dad and the store owner reached an agreement to pay it off. Dad would work for him doing carpenter jobs until the debt was paid, which he did. This resulted in a friendship between them that lasted for a very long time.

After trying his hand at red clay farming in Tenn., with very little success, Dad and Mom decided to make one more move in an attempt to provide a better life for themselves and their children. So, in the early 1950s they along with several other families from their community packed up what little possessions they had left and moved to Snyder co. Pa., where they hoped to start a new Amish community, and perhaps have an easier time at making a living. Dad often said he left Tenn. with less than he had when he got there, and when he talked about the red clay, I could detect a hint of resentment in his voice, but, in-spite of all the hardships they endured, Dad always held a deep love for the south and their way of life.

For the first two weeks, after moving to Snyder co. Pa., they lived in an old chicken house, until they found an old stone house way back off the road (now a part of State Game Lands 194). The old house was built in 1792 and neglected for many years. It was missing half of the roof and the windows, and was occupied by pigeons for many years, so in my dad's own words, "We put in new windows, fixed the roof, and shoveled out the pigeon manure." My family lived there for seven years. During that time, making a living wasn't any easier. In fact, fresh meat was scarce, so whenever old Sport, the family dog, treed a raccoon, they would have (coon) burgers for supper. This was a welcome addition to their usual meals of corn mush.

During their tenure at the old stone house, as it became known, two of my sisters, Lovina and Mary, were born. I was not to be born until they moved to a new farm, along what is now known as Clark hill road. Back then, the farm was only known as the (Wash Portzline, place), a former owner. This farm was over 100 acres, on a beautiful south facing slope, nice level fields for the most part along with enough forest land to be interesting, it had a dirt road running through the middle of it, the closest neighbor was about a half mile away, traffic was very light, and probably only three or four cars a day would go by. The purchase price was 3,400.00 and the year was 1961.

After the family was settled into the new place, life became a little less stressful for Dad and Mom. Dad began to farm, still with his old, mis-matched team, Maud and Bob. Maud was a short-legged, stocky, dark brown horse with an attitude. Bob was a long-legged, lean sorrel with a go along to get along attitude. Dad would also do odd carpenter jobs, and the older boys were old enough to be a big help, Mom was pregnant with me, but was able, along with my older sisters, to create a nice, comfortable home life for the family. Things were beginning to look up. Also, a new member to the family was a yellowish-red puppy named Tunk. He would become a huge part of my young life.

Robert Kennedy was president of the United States, the Vietnam war was in its early stages, the Cuban missile crises was dominating the news, the year was 1962. It was also the year I was born, more specifically, December 30th 1962. It was a cold winter evening when Mom told Dad that it was time, so Dad sent the younger children upstairs, and he and Mom went into the bedroom, and sometime later, I came out squalling and carrying on. This was the queue for the rest of the family to come greet me into a world of trials and personal triumphs. Dad delivered me as he had several of the other children, so he saw no reason for me to have a birth certificate, since I was, in his mind, destined to be Amish for the rest of my life and separated from what the Amish considered worldly things. But God had other plans for me, beginning with an unthinkable tragedy the following spring.

CHAPTER

2

Tragedy Strikes

I t was early 1963. I, as the newest addition to the family, was a robust, healthy baby and somewhat cute according to a letter Mom wrote to her sister Lovina on Jan. 23rd 1963. This was after taking me along to church for the first time. Here is an excerpt from the only letter I have that my mom wrote: *"Little Simon now weighs 12 pounds he's really a big boy, they all made such a fuss over him, he has dark blue eyes."*

Mom breast-fed all her children, so it only stands to reason that I was gaining weight and becoming a very healthy baby. Around that time Mom began complaining about a dull pain in her leg but passed it off as nothing serious. Besides, the doctor diagnosed it as pleurisy, so there wasn't much that could be done as a treatment. "Take it easy," was advised, but, after a few more days, the pain seemed to have traveled into her back. Sometimes she would ask one of the children to rub her back to try to relieve the pain but to no avail.

March 9th, 1963 was a normal morning. The family sat down and had breakfast. After breakfast, as was our custom, the family would gather in the living room for devotion before starting the day's activities. While they were gathering in the living room, Mom suddenly handed me over to one of the children and said she didn't feel well and laid down on the couch where she eventually passed out. Dad told my oldest brother Moses, who I believe was sixteen at the time, to go to the neighbor a mile down the road and ask him if he could take mom to a doctor. In the meantime, Dad noticed Mom had stopped breathing, so he tried to do CPR, but having no training, he really didn't understand how to perform CPR. However, out of desperation he had to try something. A few minutes later my mom went to be with Jesus, cause of death a blood clot which formed in her leg, then traveled to her heart where it lodged that fateful morning.

Immediately after Mom died, Dad turned around and looked at his eleven children, ranging from twenty years old to two-and-a-half-months old, and all he could say through his tears was, "You poor children."

In retrospect, my father never had his time to grieve. Imagine the grief and pain he had to endure at that moment. The three youngest children were four, two, and two-and-a-half months old. I was being breast-fed, so something had to be done to feed me immediately. Baby formula was probably not invented yet, so the only thing available was cow milk from a baby bottle. This I could not digest. I suffered from chronic colic and constipation. Eventually someone gave us some goats milk, which was a little better, however for the first year I didn't do very well.

The older children also had to help carry this huge burden that was dealt them. Those who weren't working away had to step up at their young age and become mothers and fathers. There were meals to cook, laundry had to be done; all the duties that a mother would do or oversee became their responsibilities. My dad had to act as a mother and father, plus he had to continue farming whenever he could, but doing carpenter work for money was impossible because he couldn't leave home. The situation began to become desperate. The unimaginable stress and responsibilities placed on everyone began to take thier toll. Without the influence of a mother to hold things together, the older children began to drift away. Dad suffered a time of depression, and the children grew even farther apart.

By the time I was two or three years old, my sisters Lydia and Elizabeth had bought a small house not far from ours. After that my memories of them are vague, at least until I was six or seven years old. My brother Moses and I never bonded much, probably because of our age difference. I am not blaming him. He endured intense pressures as well at a young age, and he had a lot of responsibilities, being the oldest boy. And I will always love and respect him for that. I did develop a closeness with Sam and Jerry during my teens. My brother Neal and I didn't get extremely close, mostly because he moved out of the house at a younger age, and he tends to be less outgoing than some of the other siblings, however, make no mistake, I love and respect all of my siblings. They all had to suffer more than they should have.

As for my sisters, Emma, Elizabeth, and Lydia, they all did their share taking care of me and other duties, however, I was simply too young to remember, and I thank them for their efforts. My fondest memories are from sister Barbara, who acted as my mother until she began working in the gladiola fields for a local farmer and picking tomatoes for Roger and Leona Hess. After that, my sister Lovina became my go to gal. Sister Mary was my playmate and got on my nerves quite often, but I love them all.

Soon after Mom died, there was a public auction somewhere nearby, so Dad decided to take some of the older girls and me along for a day out. While at the auction my sister Emma, being the oldest girl, was tasked with caring for me, so she was the one carrying me around and feeding me with a bottle, and on occasion changing my diaper. There were also many Mennonite and Amish people at the sale that day, and being a close-knit community, all of them had heard that Mom had died, so there shouldn't have been any surprise that my sister was taking care of me. It is hard to believe that even in the plain community, there are some who have no scruples and can be as vile, vicious, and the worst of the worst. This proved to be the case that day, as one of the meanest rumors known to man began to circulate throughout the plain communities. The rumor that was started that day, I believe, had a subliminal effect on how I was treated in school as a young child. This I will cover in another chapter.

Around that same time a local businessman named Hayes Stahl, whom my Father barely knew, hearing of my Father's situation came to visit him one evening with a proposal that changed our lives. This man was in the sawmill and pallet business and had more orders than he could fill. He told Dad that he had an old sawmill and power unit that he would give to Dad and help him set up if Dad would build pallets for him, thus helping him fill his orders. This would provide Dad with an income while allowing him to stay at home with the children. Of course, Dad eagerly agreed, as such an arrangement had to be heaven sent. Dad and the older boys quickly built a sawmill shed with rough lumber. Hayes then helped them set up the mill, and Dad was in business.

Dad sawed the logs into pallet lumber and the older boys nailed the pallets together. When we had enough pallets for a tractor trailer load, they would load them by hand and ship them out. The following Friday Hayes would pay Dad, then take him to the bank so he could deposit his check. This developed into a lifelong friendship between them. In fact, some of my earliest and fondest memories are of going to the bank with Hayes and my dad. The bank teller would always give me a lollipop, I would hand it to dad, and he would then break it in half so we could share it. In those days we shared everything.

In a non-related instance, someone gave me a small piece of candy, and I thought they also gave Dad a piece, so I ate mine. When I realized they hadn't given Dad one, and I hadn't shared, I felt I had betrayed him, and I cried my eyes out. It took my dad a long time to console me and convince me that it was okay. My father was everything to me.

CHAPTER

3

My Early Childhood

I would like to dedicate this chapter to my old dog, Tunk. Remember the Puppy that we acquired the year I was born? Tunk became my guardian and playmate. When I was very young and beginning to walk, I would often play in our yard adjacent to the township road. Tunk was always right by my side until I would get too close to the road. Then, he would place himself between me and the road. If I insisted on crossing the road, he would cross it with me.

There were times when I was playing in the yard that one of my siblings would come out to get me. My guardian, Tunk, would place himself between them and me, while growling menacingly, until they would tell him to knock it off. Then he would reluctantly back away. Tunk and I became inseparable. We would go on walks together in the woods when I was very young. I would become lost at times and start crying, but old Tunk would lead us home without fail. Later on, when I was old enough to hunt, we would hunt together. I was probably about fourteen years old when I saw Tunk chasing a rabbit. I noticed that he was losing ground in the chase. That is when I realized that my old friend was beginning to fail. I was overcome with sadness. When we were both sixteen, my old friend and guardian entered the happy hunting grounds, where all good dogs go, although he may not have understood it like a human. He had fulfilled the duties bestowed on him by our dear Lord, who knew that I would need a faithful friend and thus provided one for me. To this day, I have never lost my love for a good and faithful dog, and as for old Tunk, he will always own a piece of my heart.

When I was around four years old, my youngest sister Mary, who was two years older than I, started going to school. At first, I missed her terribly, because we always played together, so now I spent most of my days wandering around the farm with Tunk, waiting for her to come home. In the meantime, I played with my farm toys, underneath some big cherry trees on the lower side of the road. I had some old broken toys that my older siblings had found at the city dump. Some of the toys were homemade, like my dozer, which was a board nailed to a block of wood. This worked semi-well to make roads for my three-legged horse and a couple of beat up toy trucks with mismatched wheels.

Some days I would go upstairs in the barn and play with the rabbits and baby chickens as well. I was known to occasionally borrow a baby chick from its mother. Then, I would play mother hen, the rest of the day finding food for the chick and letting it sleep under my cupped hands, while I clucked to it. By evening, the chick had grown rather fond of me as it's surrogate mother. I would, however, always return it to its mother in the evening. I do remember enduring a number of floggings from the mother hen for my efforts. Now let's step back a bit.

Since the day Mom died, Dad would get up every morning and make breakfast for the whole family, nothing fancy, just fried potatoes and oatmeal. It was comforting to hear him whistle as he prepared breakfast in the kitchen. My older sisters would gladly have helped with breakfast, but I think Dad felt this was something he needed to do. Maybe he found it to be therapeutic, somehow. After breakfast was ready, he would open the pantry door, located underneath the steps, leading to the upstairs, where he would scratch out a tune with his fingernails. This was everyone's wake-up call. Years later, when I tore down the old house, I salvaged that particular board. It had four finger grooves worn into it, at least ¼" inch deep.

After breakfast, the older boys and Dad would go to the sawmill while some of my older sisters would leave early to pick tomatoes for the local grow-ers. The school children would be tasked with doing the dishes before they could leave for school. Dad would normally come in around noon and rustle up some grub for him and the boys. Then, everyone would return to the sawmill in the afternoon, leaving the dishes for the school children when they returned home. Supper was generally prepared by my sister Lovina, while Mary and I cleaned up the lunch dishes and swept the floors. As soon as I was old enough to hold a drying towel, I helped dry dishes. Another one of my responsibilities was to carry wood from the woodshed to the wood box beside the stove.

The rocking chair, my father rocked me in, as a child

When I was two or three years old, I would normally get hungry about 10:00, so I would wander out to the sawmill where Dad was sawing and pull on his fingers. When he leaned down to listen, I would tell him I was hungry.

He would always shut down the mill, then lead me to the house, where he would give me a piece of homemade bread, spread with apple butter. After that, he would start up the mill again and continue sawing. In the afternoon when I needed a nap, he would put me on a lumber stack on a blanket and cover me with a cage made out of fly screen, and there I would sleep to the roar of an old Detroit diesel engine, while my father kept a watchful eye on me.

The sawmill shed didn't have very many windows, so it was a little dark, especially during a dreary day. It was just such a day during deer season when I decided to open the door and take a look at several deer my brothers had shot earlier. When I cracked open that door and saw several unskinned deer hanging there in the dim light, I Imagined I saw them move, so I slammed the door shut and ran for the house. Somehow, my brothers picked up on this, because every time they were in the sawmill shed and I would venture out to be with them, they would chase me with those awful deer hides. Now I know they were just being brothers, but it did nothing to promote harmony and goodwill on my part. I just felt much safer keeping a distance from them, so I would hang out with Dad, or just keep to myself. Over time, I began to develop a liking, even a need to be alone.

In the early years, I had some close friends in our church group. They were first and second cousins, all close to my age. Our church was a typical, small Amish community. Everyone lived within walking distance from each other, I mean within three miles or so of each other. In any case, Dad would insist we walk to church. Mary and I would each grasp one of Dad's hands, and while walking, he would show us different songbirds and their songs. He would also identify trees and plants along the way. I always enjoyed walking with Dad, and I think those are still some of the best memories of my childhood.

As is customary with the Amish, we would have church every other Sunday, so on the Sundays we didn't have church, we would walk through the woods down to our grandmother's house. Dad would always take this opportunity to immerse us in nature. I began, at a very young age, to appreciate nature and the outdoors. I believe dad's nature lessons had a profound effect on my career choice later in life. And I will forever be grateful to my father for sharing his knowledge of the outdoors with us.

For the most part, I feel I had a somewhat normal childhood. I didn't really miss not having a mother, simply because I never had one. Sure I saw the other children interact with their mothers, and I often wondered how it would be to actually have a mom, however, I would soon dismiss those thoughts, because I still had my dad, and he was everything to me.

In those days, where Dad went, I went, so one Sunday when I was about five years old, a van load of us went to visit a church in Bradford Co. Pa. After the services, I was playing in the haymow with some of the other children. We were having a good time, jumping around in the hay, when all of a sudden one of the older boys came running in to tell me that he had seen my dad leaving in a van, and that they must have forgotten me. Instantly, I panicked and began screaming for Dad. I started running down the road in the direction of the van, sobbing hysterically. I ran until I couldn't run anymore. Then, I began to walk, still bawling my eyes out. Soon a horse and buggy pulled up behind me, and a man with a calming voice told me to climb in. He said he would take me to my dad. He also assured me that Dad hadn't left me, he was coming back. I didn't know the man, but the boy that told me Dad had left me was also in the buggy, so I assumed the man was his father.

As we pulled in where the church was, I saw Dad talking to some men. I assume they told him what happened, because he practically ran over to the buggy and grabbed me and held me tight for a long time. When he could finally talk, he told me he was so sorry, and that he would never, ever, abandon me. That afternoon on the way home, he explained that he saw I was playing with the other children, and one of the men wanted to show him something just a few miles down the road and he hoped to be back before I even realized that he was gone. I know that this incident weighed heavy on my dad for the rest of his life, because when my wife and I visited him, the week that he died, he again told me how much he regretted leaving me that day. I assured him, that he had made up for that many times, and that he shouldn't even think about it again. I understand what he was experiencing though, because not that many years later, I felt like I abandoned him, and I too, will carry that burden to my grave.

CHAPTER

4

A Major Change

W hen I was six years old, I started going to school. My sisters and I would walk two miles to a small, one-room schoolhouse with only one teacher for all eight grades with a total of around twenty students.

The Amish and Mennonite kids within walking distance all attended this school together. I really enjoyed going to school during the early years, especially since some of my first and second cousins also attended this school, and I had lots of friends to play with. Some of the games we played were tag or dodgeball at recess, and in later years we would play cops and robbers. I always wanted to be the cop in those days.

I wouldn't say that I was a model student by any stretch. I was your typical boy, picking on the girls, getting in arguments at times with the other boys, just the usual things that all the other students were experiencing, however when I was around nine or ten, I began to notice a change of behavior toward me, especially from some of the Mennonite kids, not all of them, just certain ones. Often when these kids were team captains picking sides I would more likely than not be the last one picked, then, the captain that got stuck with me would grimace, while reluctantly accepting me. This wasn't the only thing that happened. Often they would relentlessly mock me for things I didn't know anything about. Sometimes, the teacher would call me in and ask me why I did certain things that were against the rules. I would tell her that I had no idea what she was talking about. She would say that certain kids said they saw me do it. It became very frustrating because no matter what I said, I couldn't change her mind. Often the teacher would end up taking me to the woodshed and whipping me for something I didn't do. This only gave these kids something else to mock me with. Sadly, this continued for the remainder of my school years, only worse.

When I was twelve years old, a number of families from our church group began scouting for land in northern New York. I became very excited at the thought of possibly moving to a new location; just the thought of exploring a new location had me fired up, so I asked Dad if we were moving too. Well, he didn't know yet, he said, so I had hope. After realizing that all of my cousins were moving, I began to do the math and discovered that all the boys even near my age were moving. This meant I would be totally alone, and worse I would be the only Amish kid going to a school of Mennonites. I began to beg Dad that we should also move, but by this time he had made up his mind and the answer was a flat, NO. I clearly remember watching the last moving truck pull out and head for Norfolk, N.Y., and I began to feel a deep loneliness, along with resentment, and a resolve to someday control my own destiny.

It was during this same year, 1974, that Dad married a widow from Indiana named Esther. So, this person I had met only once before, was now my mother. What was I supposed to do with this? I didn't have a clue how to treat a mother, so imagine a twelve-year-old boy with a chip on his shoulder, first from being mistreated in school, then losing all his friends when they moved away, and now Dad giving all his attention to this new person that I was expected to call Mom. Not likely!

Esther's children from her previous marriage were all married adults, so I doubt she was looking forward to raising another kid, especially one with a bit of an attitude like I had. My brother Jerry, on the other hand, seemed to get along just fine with her. He would encourage me to try to accept her and get along with her. But I was a stubborn boy, and accepting her did not come easy. However, in later years I came to realize what a wonderful woman she was, and what a Godsend she was to my dad. I realized the personal sacrifices she made for our family, and I told her how proud I was to call her my mother.

When I returned to school the following fall as the only Amish kid, the mocking and misery continued and intensified. I would talk to Dad about it, but instead of going to the kid's parents and telling them, what for, he would look at me and quietly tell me just to turn the other cheek. That wasn't the answer I was looking for, and at one point, I told him that both my cheeks had about all they were going to take. He told me to forgive them. I didn't forgive them, not at that time anyway. I began to realize that I had no back-up. I was clearly on my own. I decided to handle things my way, so good, bad, or indifferent, my life began to develop around that philosophy.

I began to notice that when there was a group of kids, the mocking became worse, But, one on one, they actually weren't too bad to talk to, so whenever I could I would approach one of the group alone and get him to talk about anything in his personal life, then later, when he was back with the group and making fun of me, I would tell anyone who was listening what he had told me, and, if it was embarrassing enough, the group would turn on their own and leave me alone. After a while, I had enough dirt on most of them that as soon as one would try to embarrass me, I would let fly with both barrels and embarrass them unmercifully. Throughout my life, this technique developed into an ability to think on my feet and return fire with an embarrassing or smartass comeback to anyone who tried to belittle me. It wasn't the right thing to do, I know, but it sure felt good.

I came to a point where I would not tolerate any malfeasance from any of the male students unless they were a true friend of course, so when I overheard one of the students blatantly lying about me to his gang, trying to get something started, I walked up to him with a straight face and hit him with my fist as hard as I could in his stones, dropping him to his knees where he knelt hunched over bawling. When the teacher asked him what happened, he was too embarrassed to tell her, so she just stood there and glared at me for a while, then returned to her desk. That was a turning point in my life. From then on, I would defend myself, and that meant I couldn't stay with the Amish.

Around the same time, everyone else moved. Brothers Moses and Neal also moved to Norfolk, N.Y., and Brother Sam got married and moved out of the house, so that left Jerry and me at home along with two sisters Mary and Lovina. Even though Jerry was nine years older than I, we began to form a bond with each other, and I would say that he became the closest thing to a defender I ever had. We began to confide in each other and share our secrets and dreams with one another. Up to this point, I had never had such a relationship with any of my siblings, and to this day I feel we still have that bond.

Some years later in the 90s, my wonderful wife Denise and I bought an old farm in Juniata, Co. On it was an old farmhouse that needed a lot of repairs. I was doing the remodeling evenings and weekends since both of us had full time jobs. It was during this time that we decided we had saved enough money to pour cement in the basement and finally get rid of the dirt floor, and since I had very little experience with pouring cement, we hired a Mennonite man to do it for us. I won't mention his name because I don't think it would do any of us any good, but I had gone to school with him and knew him well.

One evening after I came home from work, he was still there, so we began to talk about old times, when out of the blue he asked me if I knew who my real mom was. I said sure I do, but she died when I was very young, so I don't remember her. That is when he said, "No, she didn't die. Your sister Emma is your mom," he went on to say. "Your dad is your dad, but Emma is your mom. I told him I didn't believe him, then he said that he couldn't believe that I didn't know. He said everyone knows. When I asked him who had told him, he named an older Mennonite man that I also knew quite well. After that I told him that his services were no longer needed. That evening I talked about it with Denise, and we decided to just let it go, and since this was the first time we had heard any of this maybe it would just die out. Unfortunately, that wouldn't be the case.

A number of years later, I received word that Hayes Stahl, the same man that gave Dad a sawmill years ago, was doing poorly. So, I decided to go visit him in his last days. When I got to his house an older Mennonite lady caregiver let me in and directed me to the room where Hayes was laying on a recliner. After visiting with him for a while, I noticed that his mind was failing a bit, but he knew who I was, so we talked about Dad and old times. After a while, he asked how my mom was doing. I told him she had died years ago, then he said, "No, I mean your real mom." I asked him what he meant, and he said the Mennonites told him that Emma was my real mom. I told him that it was a vicious rumor, and that I was surprised that he would believe something like that about my dad after being friends with him all these years. After that he said he didn't think it was true, but that's what they told him.

A short time later I wrote a letter to my brothers Moses and Sam and I asked them some hard questions. They both assured me unequivocally that what I heard was an old rumor that had surfaced soon after my sister Emma was seen taking care of me at a public sale, and that they had thought that by now the rumor had died out, so they never mentioned it to me. They also assured me that there was no truth to it.

And now, I might understand why I was treated so badly in school and during my teenage years. Did the parents of these school children hear this rumor and perhaps even help spread it? Undoubtedly so, and did this telegraph down to their children? More than likely. Is this the reason I was treated like a second class, citizen? I think it would be possible. If so, may the Lord have mercy on them. The pain caused by this lie is endless. This goes to show, it doesn't matter how you dress or what church you belong to. We humans are all evil at heart unless we fight against it. I want to make it clear that it doesn't matter whether you're Amish or Mennonite, there are bad apples everywhere. My desire is to forgive all involved, however it is a struggle.

CHAPTER

5

My First Attempt

There was a welding repair shop not far from the schoolhouse. This was owned by Dan Troyer, who was also a cousin to my father. Dan was a well-respected, old-order Amish man and a minister in our church. He had essentially two businesses. One was a sawmill and pallet shop, the other was the aforementioned welding shop. He employed both Amish and Mennonites in both shops. My brother Jerry worked in the welding shop as a fabricator and welder. So, for the last two years before I graduated school, I would go down to the welding shop after school and hang around with Jerry until he was ready to go home. We would then walk home together. This gave us a chance to laugh and talk about the day's events. It was while hanging out at his work that I asked him if he could teach me how to weld. He said he would, so for the next couple of years, with his guidance, I was able to master the art of welding and fabricating. I didn't get paid, nor did I expect it. I was doing it because I enjoyed making things out of steel, and especially welding.

After graduating from school with an eighth grade education, I began working at the welding shop, and I figured I had perhaps found my niche in life. I really enjoyed working there with my brother Jerry. He still watched over me and showed me some new tricks of the trade, and if I became stumped on a project, he would gladly help me out.

Even though I got along with almost everyone, there were a few people that just couldn't help but dredge up rumors they had heard from their kids, who just happened to be my old schoolmates. Then they would have a good laugh, also giving me nicknames and having an all-around good time at my expense. These events took place over several years, so during that time I kept thinking that there had to be a better way to live. I had often entertained the thought of leaving the Amish, and in my young mind I couldn't forget my dream of either joining the military or pursuing a law enforcement career, either of which I knew very little about. I really didn't have a plan for how I would go about it, though. First, I didn't have any money, which was a problem. In most Amish cultures any money you earned went to the family until you were twenty-one. After that you could begin keeping your own money, and on top of that I faced another huge problem.

When I was seventeen, several young girls about my age came to me and said that they were going to be baptized and become members of the Amish church. They wondered if I would like to join them. I thought about it for a while. I really didn't understand salvation, nor did I have a clue how to be born again. In my mind dressing Amish, following the rules, and hoping you were good was all it took, so I agreed. And so it happened, that at the ripe old age of seventeen, I was baptized and became a member in the Old Order Amish church. Now I would forever be held responsible, should I break any of their rules or leave the Amish.

The punishment for breaking rules depended on the severity. For instance, drinking an adult beverage or uttering profanity would likely result in me sitting in front of the entire church, asking the church and God to forgive me for committing these terrible sins. A second offense would land me on my knees doing the same thing. A third offense would lead to a possible shunning for up to six months. Leaving the church, however, bought you a shunning for life, or until such time that you transgressed from your wicked ways and returned to the Amish. The latter is what I was facing, should I venture to leave the Amish now.

It just so happened that when I was around seventeen, an Amish family from another church moved into our area and joined our church. This family had several boys around my age, so we palled around together and I would say we were friendly but not really friends. I found them to be somewhat undependable as friends and vaguely disloyal. In other words, I never quite trusted them, and at that stage of my life, I had learned that to maintain a true friend, I had to have an unfettered loyalty toward that friend, and I demanded the same. If any friend ever broke that loyalty, they immediately became an acquaintance.

One day the oldest boy and I began to talk about leaving the Amish, mostly just feeling each other out, neither one trusting the other completely. We decided that we would have to tolerate each other if we wanted to succeed in our escape. He had a contact in another state that would help us if we could only get there. The plan was to catch the greyhound bus and travel to his contact, however we needed someone to run cover for us at home until we were able to safely depart. He came up with a not so brilliant plan to recruit his younger brother for this task. I wasn't too excited to have not one but two disloyal friends involved, but we confronted him about it anyway, and he seemed all for it, even made us promise that if we succeeded, we would come back for him.

On the planned evening of escape this boy and I met at a pay phone where he began making final preparations with his contact, and our little plan seemed like it might happen. We were starting to feel a little hopeful that we might actually get out of there undetected, when all of a sudden, all heck broke loose, the door flew open, and his Dad stormed in, grabbed him by the arm, and yanked him out of the phone shack, then, frog marched him to his buggy, and should I say, helped him get on it, (he was at least twenty years old). I was scared and I was eighteen. I ran outside and there was my brother Jerry. All he said was, "Dad would like you to come home." I was fresh out of options, so I complied. Then, while we walked, we talked. I told Jerry that he of all people should know what I have to endure here, and someday I would leave. All he said was, "I know."

Turns out this boy's younger brother, who was my age, couldn't take the pressure and told his dad. His dad in turn sent a boy to tell my dad, and thus our dreams were shattered, at least temporarily. A few days later, I had a go at the young man that betrayed us. I vaguely remember clutching his throat with both hands and explaining the concept of loyalty to him in no uncertain terms. I was seldom given to violence, but that day was an exception.

Many years later the boy that had teamed up with me made his escape and became a successful over the road truck driver. I, on the other hand, was about to have a second go at it.

Meanwhile, my father, being the bishop of our church, consulted with the rest of the elders, and they decided that since we had not actually left the Amish during our failed attempt, they would not place the ban on us. Instead, they would leave us off with a stern warning. In the meantime, I was contemplating my second attempt.

Several months earlier, a young man named Sammy moved in from Missouri to live with his sister and brother-in-law. He had a reputation of living fast and loose, too reckless for my liking, so being friends with him was not on my bucket list, to say the least. However, several months after my first attempt at leaving, he approached me and asked if it was true that I had tried to leave. At first, I figured he was just trying to get information so he could poke fun at me in front of the other boys, so I tried to deflect his question and go about my business, but he kept hounding me about it. After a while, he said that he was planning to leave but that he would like someone to go with him, and he asked if I would be interested. I told him how I had been betrayed the last time, and that if I would ever go again, I would rather go alone. He said he understood, but he had a plan that he thought might work. I could detect a sincerity in his voice, so I agreed to hear his plan.

He said that he knew an English farmer in Missouri, that he had worked for previously, so he was sure that he could get a job there again, and he thought he could get a job for me as well, at least for a while. He also knew a boy that had left the Amish a few years prior that would let us stay with him at his trailer until we could get our own place to live. I had to admit this plan sounded a tad better than the last plan that was presented to me, so I agreed to give it a go. (Here is where I went astray.)

I still had no money. So, when I got my paycheck at the end of the week, I told them to make it out to me instead of Dad, that way I could cash it. Now I had a little over 200 dollars in my pocket.

The next morning, I believe it was a Saturday. Sammy and I met down along the, Susquehanna River, which was adjacent to Route 11&15, a four-lane highway. We were going to attempt to flag down a greyhound bus and leave. However, we couldn't stand brazenly along the road for fear someone would see us. So, we lay on the riverbank, hoping we would see the bus approach. Our plan was to run out in time to flag it down. Needless to say, we missed the bus.

After laying along the riverbank until dusk, Sammy came up with a plan. He would call a friend he felt sure would be friendly to our cause and ask him if we could stay at his place for the night. We would then ask him if he would take us to the bus station in a nearby town. His idea sounded plausible, so I agreed. He then ran across the road to a pay phone and called. Soon, his friend arrived and took us to his place.

That night I couldn't sleep. I knew my dad was worried sick by now, and it was breaking my heart, but I knew if I wanted to succeed, I had to endure. The next morning the man took us to the bus station and dropped us off. We bought our tickets to Bowling Green Missouri. We still had some time to kill, so we went to a used clothing store, and I bought a pair of well-worn jeans, a shirt, and an old Army jacket. After that, we ditched our Amish clothes in a trash can. At that moment I began to feel something come over me. Oh yeah, I believe it was a taste of freedom.

The bus ride to Missouri was fairly uneventful. I felt an excitement unlike anything I had ever felt before, but there was also a dark cloud of apprehension hanging over me. I didn't have much money left. I also didn't know any of these people Sammy knew. What if they didn't give me a job? What would I do then? So I began to devise a plan B, just in case everything went south. I thought perhaps I would Try to join the Air Force. Little did I realize that I was in no way qualified in my present state. However, I began to feel a little better knowing that my destiny was in my own hands, or so I thought, years later I realized, that my destiny was never in my hands, but in God's hands. His plan for me was far bigger than I could imagine.

When we arrived in Bowling Green, Sammy's friend, the one we were going to stay with, came to pick us up. He didn't seem particularly happy to see us, and I suspected we weren't all that welcome, but he agreed to let us crash at his trailer for the time being. That day, Sammy contacted his farmer friend and he agreed to give Sammy work and he said he would give me a try. That same day, Sammy called his sister's neighbor back home and asked if they could tell our folks where we were, and that we were okay. After that, I felt better knowing Dad would know that I was alive. The next day, the farmer picked us up and took us to his farm, where we worked on a fence all day. That evening the farmer's wife gave us our first real haircuts. After that I felt truly free.

We worked for the farmer for several days. Then one morning, he told Sammy he was sorry but he just didn't have enough work for two people, so I had to stay at the trailer that day. That evening I told Sammy that I was going to try to join the Air force. I couldn't believe it when Sammy tried his best to talk me out of it. Of all the things Sammy was willing to do without regret, it seemed where he drew the line was joining the Military. Unbeknownst to me, Sammy made another phone call home, this time to tell them that they should come and get me because I was going to join the Military.

Several days later I was at the trailer alone when a van pulled up outside. Imagine my surprise when out steps my dad and my brother-in-law Ben. I went to the door and they asked if they could come in. I said yes, then we sat at the table and talked. Dad asked if I was alright, I said I was, then he said that I was welcome to come along home with him if I wanted to, but I would have to decide that on my own. He also said that he would return the following day to hear what I had decided. I thanked him for coming and told him I would think it over.

That night when Sammy came back from the farm, I berated him a bit for dropping the dime on me. I wasn't terribly mad at him though, because he actually thought he was doing me a favor. That night I gave it some deep thought, and eventually I decided that I really couldn't see a way forward, not in my present state. What I dreaded the most, though, was going back to the same life I had left. I decided I would ask Dad for permission to go to Norfolk, N.Y. and stay with my sister Lovina and her husband for a while. There I would be with all my cousins and old friends that had moved away in 1974. I also began to second guess my decision to leave the Amish. Nothing seemed to be working in my favor. Suddenly it occurred to me that both times I had teamed up with another person, and both times the other person seemed to be the reason I failed. It wasn't all their fault. I had to take some of the blame, but I was sure that if I could rely on my own instincts I would succeed. Not having any money was my biggest issue, so I decided that for the time being I would put leaving on the back burner, at least until I turned twenty-one.

The next morning when Dad and Ben arrived, we talked about what I had decided, and I told Dad that I would be willing to return, but I would like to go to N.Y. if it would be alright with him. It is not common for a child to be allowed to move out of their parents' house before the age of twenty-one, but under these circumstances Dad agreed to try it, so I said I would go. Dad then gave me some of my Amish clothes that he had brought along, but no hat. When I said I didn't have a hat, Ben gave me his hat, a kind and generous act that I will never forget. After I decided to return, Sammy decided that he wanted to return as well. In later years Sammy made another run at leaving and succeeded. He lived in Idaho until his death a few years ago.

The next morning, Dad and I boarded a greyhound bus headed back to Pa. While riding on the bus, I spent hours looking out the window, wondering what direction my life would go next. I began to think that maybe I wasn't cut out for anything other than an Amish life. Immediately my eyes would tear up and I would get a heavy feeling in my chest, but, when I allowed myself to imagine a different life, I began to feel much better. I decided that I would not give up the dream, but instead, I would take a few years to plan and try to pick a better route. I decided to read books about the military and try to learn as much as I could about the requirements for joining. I had to do this in complete and total secrecy in order not to raise any suspicions.

During the next three years, being Amish wasn't all bad. There were even times that perhaps the right girl could have convinced me to remain Amish, however deep inside there was a nagging feeling of discontent that never left me.

After returning to Pa. with Dad, I had to brace myself for some form of punishment from the church. I certainly wasn't looking forward to this. The first Sunday after we got back, the members, minus Sammy and I, had a meeting after the services to decide what our fate should be. There were some that wanted to ban or shun us out of hand, but the majority decided that if we would confess our sins on our knees in front of the whole church, it would suffice, so confess we did. I thought they left us off easy, considering we had nice haircuts, and there was no visible contrition exuding from either one of us. In fact, after seeing just a hint of envy in some of other boys, we became a little cocky about the whole thing.

A few months later, after things had returned to normal, Dad came through on his promise to allow me to go to N.Y. and live with my sister for a while, so I packed some belongings and was able to catch a ride to Norfolk N.Y.

News travels fast among the Amish churches, and unbeknownst to me, I was labeled a flight risk by every church within letter-writing distance, including the church in Norfolk, N.Y., so the preachers there considered me a loose cannon and were afraid that I might influence some of their young folks to flee. They were well aware that any crack in their armor would make controlling their subjects that much harder, so even before I arrived, they had the long knives out for me.

CHAPTER

6

Life in N.Y.

When I arrived at my sister Lovina and her husband's house, they provided a room for me in their unfinished upstairs. The room was warm, and it had a bed of sorts, also a dresser with an open front. The room didn't have any doors yet, but it was semi-private and comfortable. There was a downside though, to living with them, because their home was way outside the Amish community, and I didn't have a horse and buggy, so traveling to the young folks, gatherings, or to my cousin Joe's place, who happened to be my best friend, became a bit of an issue. However, most times when I couldn't catch a ride with someone, my brother-in-law would allow me to take his horse and buggy. I didn't like to do that though because his horse had bad feet and could easily end up lame, so it was best not to drive her more than necessary.

Soon after arriving in N.Y., I was able to get a job at the Amish cheese factory, where my cousin Joe also worked, so it became easier to just go home with him sometimes, that way I could ride to work with him in the morning. This worked out well for me, but didn't please my brother-in-law too much. It seemed that he thought he should be keeping an eye on me, and hopefully, prevent me from entering into sin. And my coming and going without his knowledge of where I was or what I was doing didn't sit well with him, so we had a number of conversations, Mostly he conversed, and I listened. Now that he was married, he became a very strict and somber Amish man and was quick to lower the boom, so to speak, on anyone who committed the same transgressions that he committed as a young man. He wasn't atypical in this regard; stabbing one another in the back is very common among some Amish.

While working at the cheese factory I came to know an old Mohawk Indian named Harry. He was retired from the Railroad. But for extra income, he would haul the Amish on short runs to town. He would show up at the cheese factory every morning just in case we needed parts from somewhere, or if one of us needed to go to town he would take us, for a fee.

Harry just so happened to be a close neighbor to my brother-in-law, so I began to stop at his house after work evenings to visit a while before going on home. It wasn't long until Harry and I became good friends. We would sit beside the old wood stove and indulge in an adult beverage or two while his wife Hilda made supper. They would always invite me to stay, and sometimes I would, depending on how many beers Harry consumed before supper, Harry would become somewhat aggressive after consuming five or six adult beverages, and me being partial to my scalp, I would keep a careful count of his empty bottles. After he tossed bottle number four into a fifty-five gallon steel drum beside the stove, I would bid him and Hilda goodnight, and head for home. The next morning Harry was back to his normal jovial self, and neither one of us would ever mention the night before.

Harry drove an old ford pick-up truck, and one of his chief complaints was the lack of a cassette player in the radio. So, when he heard that I was returning to Pa. to visit Dad and my stepmother, he asked if I would keep an eye open for a radio cassette player for his truck. I told him that there was an old junk yard in Pa. close to the home place, and that I would try to find one suitable for his truck, which I did.

After getting back to my sister's place in N.Y., I placed the player on my dresser with the intention of giving it to Harry after work that day. I even told him that I would help him install it that evening. When I got back to my room, I noticed the player was gone. I couldn't understand why someone would take a radio designed for a vehicle, so I asked my brother-in-law if he knew what happened to it. He said he smashed it with a sledgehammer. He then proceeded to warn me that such a sin would most certainly land me in hell, and that is why he took it upon himself to smash it, and, he said that I might have to confess my sin to the church. I then told him that I had brought it along for Harry because he asked me for one. After stammering around for a while, he said he didn't care, just being in possession of it is a sin. At that moment I was about as mad as I could be. The fact that he went into my bedroom snooping around, then breaking my belongings without first asking me about it, really aggravated me, I couldn't entirely blame him for his actions, though, The whole Amish system depends on intimidation to maintain control of its subjects, so for him, it was a simple case of being indoctrinated by a long line of Amish ancestors. He really didn't know another way, however, this didn't sit well with me, so I began staying with my cousin Joe whenever possible.

Joe and I were alike in some respects. We both enjoyed an adult beverage now and again. I'm not talking getting drunk, we never even did that, I'm talking drinking one beer while in an out of the way location, say, on a walk, or along the railroad tracks. We did this not because we really liked beer, because neither one of us really did. I think we both liked the thrill of a little rebellion, let's just say, a small taste of freedom.

It was during one of these single beer forays that one of the not so trustworthy boys walked up on us and caught us red handed. At that moment we knew he was going to tell the bishop on us, and sure enough, that following week the bishop asked if Joe and I would stop at his place some evening. We knew what it was about, and neither one of us were prone to lying, so we readily admitted to having one beer. He was actually very understanding and kind, but he said we would have to confess to the church our sin of drinking a beer, not that it was so wrong he said, but just to keep the peace.

Now, unlike me, Joe was prone to be a lot more acceptable of the Amish rules and customs. Let's just say he was known as a pretty good boy. It really aggravated him that he had to confess to the church for the high crime and misdemeanor of drinking a single beer. This was also his very first confession, which was devastating to him. I however, was getting quite accustomed to this type of treatment, and was able to, more or less, shrug it off. He was so uncomfortable about it that I began to feel sorry for him, until, to my surprise, while hanging out in his bedroom on the morning when our confession was due, he reaches under his little dresser and pulls out two beers. After handing one to me, he grumbled, "If I'm gonna have to do this, it's gonna be for two beers." I began to grin as we toasted one another and finished them off.

The first year of living in N.Y. went rather well in my opinion. I enjoyed working at the cheese factory and living at cousin Joe's place. Joe's mother was a sister to my dad, and as far as I was concerned, she was the kindest and most God-fearing lady I had ever known. Her husband was a bit older than she was, and almost deaf. He paid almost no attention to me, so I was sure he disliked me. I tried to avoid him at all costs. He was a man of very few words, and when he spoke, I always imagined he must have sounded like God speaking to Moses on the mountain. I felt lucky to be alive after the first sentence. Later, I realized that he wasn't an unkind man, that it was his inability to hear that made him seem unapproachable. A few years after I left N.Y., my aunt was losing her battle with cancer, so I went up to see her, and was truly humbled when I saw my uncle caring for her in the kindest and gentlest of ways until her death.

I made a lot of friends while in N.Y. and got along with most of them, however, there were some young boys that liked nothing better than getting someone in trouble. One such family of boys lived just outside the town of Norfolk, and often we would see the younger ones hanging around in town. Their dad was known to make a lot of wine which he consumed at home. He even had a red nose with protruding blood vessels that we figured was caused by an overconsumption of alcohol. And, because the boys were always looking to stab someone in the back, we tried our best to avoid them.

One evening my cousin Peter and I were walking through town, and for some reason Peter needed to make a phone call. The nearest pay phone was just inside the door of the saloon, so after contemplating it for a while, Peter decided it would be safe to step inside and make a quick phone call, while I stood guard. Not wanting to draw attention waiting outside, I bailed through the door with him, and while he was making his call, I was nervously watching out the window. All of a sudden, the window went dark, and a face appeared with cupped hands around his eyes, peering in at us. I immediately recognized the face as belonging to one of the aforementioned, back-stabbing boys. We figured we would have to explain our actions to the bishop, but, surely, there wouldn't be any action taken against us. After all, we were only using the phone—wrong! We had to confess our massive sin of using a phone inside a bar, this, in the sitting position. By now, I was starting to get my fill of this kind of treatment.

A while after the bar incident, Peter and I devised a most brilliant plan to get even with these backstabbing boys and teach them a valuable lesson. Our plan would be executed the next Sunday evening at the young folks gathering. I was to buy a six-pack of (near) beer. This was a non-alcoholic beverage that tasted like beer. I would then park my horse and buggy a little apart from everyone else, just to make sure to be noticed. Later, Peter and I would stand by my buggy and drink a few cans while tossing the empties on the ground, knowing full well the backstabbing boys would see us, then turn us in for drinking beer. Our defense would be that it's non-alcoholic, therefore, it's not against the rules, and the joke would be on them. Everything went exactly as planned. We knew if they saw us drinking something, they would investigate after we left, which they did.

A few days later we were told to stop at the bishop's place. Peter and I were actually looking forward to this visit. We figured we had this one in the bag. Surely after we show him that it wasn't real beer, the bishop would laugh a little and tell us to go on home. In fact, we were laughing at the thought of poking a little fun at the back-stabbing boys the next time we saw them. So, after giving our side of the story to the bishop, we offered to show him a can to prove there was no alcohol in it, but to our surprise he wasn't interested in seeing it. He said that several of the church members didn't care about the alcohol, or lack of alcohol. They were convinced that we sinned just by pretending it was beer, and he said that to keep peace and good harmony in the church, we would have to confess our sin, in the sitting position. At that moment I began to see the light. It seemed that anytime I was involved in an infraction, guilty or not, I would be forced to confess. It was at this point that I began to develop a low tolerance for their stupidity. It seemed to me that most of the non-biblical rules were just plain dumb.

As is customary in the Amish churches, if you are accused of a sin, you would be asked to step outside after services while the members gave witness, if there were any witnesses, then they would ask if there were any members opposed to punishing the offenders. It took only two members to oppose the punishment, and the whole thing would be stopped. According to my informant on the inside, while we were dismissed several members took it upon themselves to bear false witness, telling the congregation that near beer has at least 9% alcohol, and insisted we should give our confession on our knees. After a while, one of the members came outside and told us to come on in. After taking our seats, the bishop informed us that we were to make a confession on our knees for drinking beer.

We knew that to refuse could easily have resulted in a shunning for six months, or until such time, that we would truly repent. So, having few options, we did as we were instructed, almost. I, however, changed my wording to non-alcoholic near beer, and no one even tried to correct me. They could see that I was at the end of my rope, and 100% unrepentant. There were members present that knew better, but didn't speak up, and there were others that straight up lied as witnesses. Ironically, almost forty years later, I still remember who they were. I have forgiven them, so I won't mention their names. By now, I was getting a clear and unfavorable vision of the Amish church and its method of controlling their members, no matter what the cost.

It was also customary among the Amish to ask some of the young single men to do chores for them while on vacation. Most of the time we only had to feed a few horses, maybe a dog and some cats. Normally the families going on vacation would allow us to stay at their house at night and cook breakfast, and then go to work afterwards. This would save us a lot of travel time, and, it is worth mentioning, that we never asked for payment of any kind, and never received any to my knowledge. Joe and I were often asked to do this because we worked and traveled together, and we didn't have a lot of chores ourselves because of working at the Cheese factory. We did sort of enjoy it because it gave us a chance to play bachelor and cook what we wanted. Basically it resulted in a few nights of freedom.

One such time we were asked to chore for a family with a herd of dairy cows. At first we were a little reluctant, knowing full well that milking twelve cows by hand, morning and evening, plus taking care of the horses was going to take several hours. We were concerned that we wouldn't be able to get to the cheese factory in time for the milk delivery, and being late was not an option. Even though we didn't want to do it, we thought it was our Christian duty to help them out (mostly Joe thought that). This just happened to be one of the men that brought false witness against me in the near beer incident, and I didn't feel particularly loyal toward him. Joe however, being the good boy that he was, reminded me that here was a chance for me to return good for evil, and he thought we should do it, so, I agreed to do it this one time.

The next evening we stopped at the dairy farm after work so the man could show us how to do his chores. To me it seemed like an awful lot to get done, and still make it to work on time. I could see by the look on Joe's face that he was having reservations himself, but we had given our word already, and backing out wasn't an option, but then things started getting a lot worse. The man said that his wife didn't want us to stay at their house while they were gone. She didn't like the idea of someone sleeping in their beds. Also she didn't want to return to a messy house. It would be an understatement to say that Joe and I weren't a little taken aback by this arrangement. This meant we would have to travel by horse and buggy, six miles from Joe's house to the dairy farm, then chore for two and a half hours, then travel another six miles to the cheese factory, and be there by 7:00 AM. After we left the farm and started home, I told Joe, "So much for returning good for evil." He didn't say a word.

The next morning we got up extremely early and drove an hour to the dairy farm. Joe being the fastest at milking tore right into the milking. I fed the numerous horses and bottle-fed the calves. After that I would help Joe finish up milking the cows. Then we cleaned the milk house and turned the livestock out to pasture. Only after all that were we ready to drive another hour to work. After arriving at the cheese factory we would eat a few slices of cheese for breakfast, then that evening we would do it all over again.

The next morning, we decided that we had to do something else. This arrangement was not going to work for an entire week, so we decided that we were going to have to sleep at the farm and we figured we could fry some eggs for breakfast, and just clean up before they were scheduled to come home. We knew that getting the milking done was more important than not sleeping in their house, so, for the rest of the week we slept on the couch and on a blanket on the floor, but wouldn't you know it. The day before they were scheduled to come home, at approximately 03:00 AM, the door burst open and a pile of kids swarmed in, followed by their parents. Not only were we rudely awakened, but we were also caught red handed, sleeping in their house. You would have thought we had committed a capital crime. The wife was screaming at us, the husband, in the most un-Christian like fashion ordered us outside and told us how ignorant we were for not listening. He did give us two options though, which was nice of him. We could either go home or we could sleep in the barn until morning. He never bothered to thank us for all the work we had done, just kicked us out. Needless to say, my loyalty to him really hadn't gotten any stronger, and I believe it would be fair to say that Joe felt approximately the same way. I began to wonder why anyone would want to be part of a so-called Christian church that allowed their members to be that ignorant. I dare say at that moment a small spark inside became a small flame, once again.

CHAPTER

7

Time is Running Out

By now, I had been living in N.Y. about one year, and already I had been forced to confess my sins in church at least three times, and I was getting tired of it. I again began to seriously contemplate leaving the Amish. I knew I needed to wait until I was at least twenty-two years old. The reason for that was I was still sending the money I earned home to my Dad. I did keep a little petty cash for my own expenses, but I wasn't allowed to keep the money I earned until I turned twenty-one, so I figured by the time I turned twenty-two years old, I should have some money saved up, but in the meantime I began to put a plan together.

Several days later, I hitchhiked to a nearby town where I knew there was an Army recruiting station. After walking up to the recruiting station, I took a good look around just to make sure no one was watching. The coast was clear, so I dashed through the door, and there sitting behind a desk was an Army Sgt. with a look on his face somewhere between total shock and disbelief. There I stood in total Amish dress and looking very much out of place.

He seemed to be at a loss for words, so I blurted out, "What do I have to do to join the Army?"

He hesitated just for a moment while he regained his composure, then he asked if I have a GED or high school diploma. Of course I didn't and told him so. He then informed me that I would have to get one before I could join. I guess he saw the disappointed look on my face, because as I turned to go, I heard him say, "Wait, you also need to take an ASVAB test."

He explained that it was an "Armed services vocational aptitude battery," and passing it was required by everyone who joined any branch of the service. He also said that he could give me a practice test, that way I would know what areas I would have to improve on. I was a little apprehensive but told him I would have a go at it, so he sat me down at a desk and laid a bunch of questions in front of me, then he said that it was a timed test and that I have fifteen minutes to answer as many of the questions as I can. He hit the timer and I began to cipher.

After the allotted time had passed, he gathered up my answers and began to grade them. When he turned around to give me my score he had a slight grin on his face. He then told me that I did a lot better than he expected. He pointed out a few areas for me to work on but said I shouldn't have a problem passing the real test when I decide to take it. At that moment I was on cloud nine. I knew that with a little work I would be able to achieve my dream, my confidence was already beginning to grow, and now I had a path forward. I got up and thanked him for his time, then walked out the door. As I closed the door, I heard him say, "Good luck, you'll do fine." I could feel that flame burning a little hotter. I felt that nothing could stop me now.

I continued to work at the cheese factory, as if nothing was going on, but in my mind a plan was starting to take shape. Now, it wasn't all I thought about all the time, but it was always in the back of my mind, and any time that I could gather any information from someone without raising suspicions I would do so and store it to memory. There was a girl named Mary, working at the cheese house when I started. She would take care of the sales counter and help out in production when sales got slow. I would say hi to her and try to have a conservation at times but could never extract more than a few words out of her before she just simply walked away. I did notice that she seemed to get along okay with cousin Joe, so I asked him if I had done something wrong. He said, "No it's not you, she just has to get to know someone before she trusts them." Well, I could relate to that, so I just kept having small conversations with her and over time I began to notice a change in her. She began telling me things about her family, and I told her some of my experiences, and after a while we began to develop a trusting friendship with each other. Over a period of time, she became one of the most loyal friends I had ever had to that point. I trusted her enough to even tell her of my plans to leave the Amish. She said it wouldn't be her choice, but she could easily see why I would have my fill of the Amish. She promised me she would keep it a secret.

Joe was also a loyal friend, but I could never confide in him about my plans to leave. Joe was loyal to me, but he held an even deeper loyalty to the Amish church and their system, so to entrust him with my plans was out of the question. His conscience would simply have forced him to try to bring a stop to my plans somehow, and I knew that, so I didn't want to put him in a position where he had to make that choice. One of my core values pertaining to loyalty was to always protect your loyal friends, even if at great personal cost. This is what I practiced, and I expected the same.

During my last year in N.Y., the Bishops began to connive a way to force me to return to Pa. I don't believe they had the authority to do that, but then why let that stop them? The leader was my stepmother's brother. He was also my friend Mary's Grandfather. He approached Mary and several others one day and asked them how they would feel about it if the bishops forced me to go home. Mary vehemently opposed the idea, as did some of the others. After this the idea was dropped. That's what loyalty means to me.

Now Mary and I were never more than friends. I always suspected she and Joe had a special fondness for each other, and sure enough, it wasn't long until they began dating. This caused some hardship for me, especially Sunday evenings after the young folks gatherings. Normally I would ride with Joe to his house for the night, and then to work the next morning, now however, I was forced to either hitch a ride with someone or borrow my brother-in-law's horse and buggy. I didn't like doing that because that meant I would have to return to his house for the night, which I didn't enjoy, and then walk to the cheese factory the next morning. I wasn't particularly fond of this arrangement, but unfortunately, it was the hand I was dealt, so I learned to adapt, until I returned to Pa. several months later.

Meanwhile, I heard through my brothers Sam and Jerry that Dad's church in Pa. was experiencing some difficulty due to some members adopting a different view of salvation. They were sure that the church was heading for a split because of this, and they thought that maybe it would be a good idea if I would return home in the hope that doing so would relieve some stress on Dad. I was well aware of what this so-called strange belief could do to an Amish church. I had seen it before in other churches. It almost always ended in a split, and those who split away almost always ended up getting cars and joining other churches who were generally more liberal than the old order Amish. The Amish would then place them in the ban and shun them, which resulted in families being split, and as a result, hard feelings generally followed.

Now you're wondering, what kind of a belief could this strange belief be to cause such strife among such a forgiving and peace-loving church as the old order Amish? I will try to explain it in a nutshell, The Amish believe that you must be born again. No problem there, right? But then through faith and self-denial (in essence, the Amish lifestyle), you hope for salvation through Jesus Christ. See Romans,8; 24-25, (NKJV).

The Amish believe in hope of salvation, because the testament almost always speaks of salvation in future tense, such as, "You will be saved." Thus you can only receive the gift of salvation after you die, but until then, you have hope of salvation through the blood of Christ. One other thing that guides the Amish is 2nd, Cor: 6, 15-17, (NKJV) where the Apostle Paul instructs his church to separate themselves from unbelievers. Now, somewhere along the line this simple statement, to the Amish, came to mean separating themselves from the world, and the only way that they could have adopted this stance would be to believe that anyone who isn't Amish must be an unbeliever. To me this is a dangerous place to be. On the flip side, those who accept the (strange belief), believe that when you accept Jesus Christ as your savior, you have assurance of salvation. Even though the promise of salvation is future tense, they generally feel comfortable saying they are saved, as in already. That is the part that doesn't sit well with the Amish.

Most times when a former Amish person becomes saved, they will also begin studying the bible more, and by doing so they soon realize that separating yourselves from worldly things is done in your heart, as opposed to things not accepted by the Amish church. In fact, they soon understand that owning cars is not a sin in and of itself, instead they are just material things. Read Romans, 14, 13-23, (NKJV). Understand, of course, that you can sin with a car, depending what you do with it, just like a buggy can also be used for sin. Now the buggy and the car are not able to sin. They don't know any better. The one is wood and canvas, the other is recycled soda cans, depending what country it's made in. So, it stands to reason that the one committing sin, most likely, would be the driver, right? So where does his or her sin most likely originate from? I would assume from their heart.

So, by now you are beginning to understand why the Amish church has such a fear of the (strange belief). Nothing will demolish the age-old Amish belief and system of control faster and more thoroughly than having their members realize that what they were indoctrinated with all their lives isn't even biblical. And that is why, for many years, Amish parents, in hushed tones, have warned their children of the devils (strange belief).

I thought about what was going on in my home church and the stress that was being placed on my father. I knew that he would do everything he could to prevent a split, but I also knew he would be under tremendous pressure from neighboring Bishops to lower the boom, so to speak, in the hopes of preventing this strange belief from spreading to other churches.

So after considering all my options, I realized that at this point in my life, it really didn't matter all that much where I was living. I figured that my plans could be executed as easily from Pa. as from N.Y. Perhaps there would be even be a way to capitalize from the confusion going on in Pa. Understand, I am not a malicious person at heart. I pitied my Father for what he was going through. In no way was I trying to capitalize from his pain, but I fully understood that no matter when I left the Amish, his heart was going to be broken, and that is the only regret I would ever have for leaving the Amish. The fact that I caused my father such pain. Several months later I decided to return to Pa., so I said goodbye to my N.Y. friends and rode the old Grey Hound bus to Pa. I was twenty years old.

CHAPTER

8

A Dream Comes True

A while before I moved to N.Y., my two brothers, Sam and Jerry, each purchased a half of the home farm from Dad. Jerry was still single and living at home, but Sam was married, with several children, so he purchased the half with the buildings. Dad, my stepmother, Jerry, and I along with my two youngest sisters, Lovina and Mary, moved to a small house adjacent to the farm. This was the same house that several of my sisters had lived in when I was very young. By the time I moved back my two sisters were married. In fact, Lovina and her husband lived in N.Y. where I stayed part of the time. Mary and her husband David still lived in Pa., as did my sister Lydia and her husband George, along with sister Emma and her husband Jake.

After I returned home from N.Y., I was able to get a job at the same welding shop as before. Unfortunately, many of the same Amish and Mennonites that worked there before were still there, and it didn't take me long to realize that they hadn't changed much from their mocking and fun-making ways towards me. But now I was older, and less likely to be intimidated. Soon, I was firing back with both barrels. This didn't put a stop to it, but it did slow it down some.

At that time, I, along with most of the men there, chewed tobacco of some form or the other, and as was customary if a person ran out, you would ask one of the others for a chew to hold you over until you could purchase some, Most of the guys would freely give you a chew. Some would hem and haw around, then reluctantly share their can with you. So, imagine my surprise when one of the reluctant ones approached me one day and offered his can to me without me asking for it. I should have been suspicious, but being a little naïve, I accepted. Soon after that everyone began to ask me how that horse manure tasted. At first, I didn't believe them, but one person I trusted said, "You know, that chew was mixed with horse manure". Soon everyone in the shop knew it and the fun-making was relentless. Needless to say I felt betrayed and hurt.

That evening when I saw the offending person enter the horse barn to get his horse, I slipped in behind him and tackled him to the ground, which was covered in horse manure, I was having a serious adrenaline rush, as I picked up a juicy horse biscuit and smashed the entire thing into his mouth. Then I picked up another hand full and smashed it across his entire face. I noticed he was beginning to choke on horse manure, so I let him up and told him this was just a taste of what I would do to him if he ever tried anything like that again. Then I walked out. Like I said before, I was seldom given to violence, but I fully intended to defend myself.

Sometime during the year that I turned twenty-one and was able to start keeping my own money, I purchased a cheap horse and built myself a buggy. I wouldn't have spent my money on these things, but without them I didn't have a way to get around.

One Sunday evening, some young folks from a more liberal Amish church came to our gathering. I say more liberal because their church allowed farm tractors and skid loaders, and they dressed much nicer than we did. Among those young folks was a young girl that simply could not be ignored, so with some coaxing from the other guys, I actually asked her on a date. Soon we were dating steady. I would hire a driver to take me to her mom and dad's place about every two weeks. Then, after seeing her for the weekend, the driver would pick me up and take me home again.

During this time, I had many misgivings. I still had the dream to leave the Amish. The other thing I knew was if we ever were to get married, I couldn't move to her church without being shunned because of their tractors, etc. The alternative was that she would have to move to our church and leave all those frills behind. I was embarrassed at the way we lived and would have felt sorry for her if she had to move to our church. She was a very nice girl and would probably have done it without complaint, but I decided that I couldn't put her through that, so after about three months of dating, I told her our situation just wouldn't work out, so we stopped dating. Maybe I was being selfish, I don't know. I know one thing, I felt like a real jack-ass for a long time afterwards.

Meanwhile the strange belief was still taking its toll on the church. Several families had left and joined other churches. My sister Lydia and her husband were one of them. They joined a Baptist church right out of the gate. Others were inclined to join less liberal, black-car churches, then work their way up to more liberal churches over time. The bishops and ministers were starting to get very worried, which resulted in everyone being watched very closely. One misstep and you would be under suspicion and questioned.

It was during this time that several of us younger men owned revolvers. There was no church rule saying we couldn't own one, so we didn't think there would be a problem. We even went to the trouble to get carry permits just to make sure we weren't breaking the law. I had a small revolver that I used to dispatch animals while trapping for furs. I didn't flaunt it, because I knew Dad didn't care for any kind of handgun. Sometimes, I would keep it in my coat pocket, which I hung in the hallway. One day, Dad must have felt it in my coat, because that evening, he confronted me about it. I told him that I had it for trapping. He said that it was wrong to have it, and that I would have to confess to the church. I told him that since there was no rule saying I couldn't have a pistol, I didn't see how he could make me confess. He wouldn't hear of it and threatened me with a more severe punishment if I didn't comply. I couldn't think of a reason why he would be so quick to want to punish me, especially in church, and for something that wasn't even against any rules.

The following Sunday Dad was going to bring the handgun issue up to the members, then decide on the severity of the punishment. So, after the services, I was asked to go outside and wait until someone came out to get me. I was seething mad when I went outside. I didn't have the guts to just go home, but I figured they were going to have to look for me. So, I went out behind the barn and stood behind a tree, I simply couldn't believe that this was happening to me again, and at that moment, I made myself a promise that this was going to be the last time.

After a while, I saw someone come out on the porch and look around, then he went around the house looking for me. Soon he ran back inside. A few minutes later, four more guys came running outside and began to scatter out around the buildings. One of them was my brother Jerry. After a while, brother Jerry approached to within speaking distance from me, so I called out to him. He seemed very worried, and I couldn't help but pity him a little. He was the only person that felt I was being railroaded, but there wasn't anything he could do about it. I told him that I would go in, but that this would be the last time any Amish church would ever treat me this way. He said, "I know."

As I walked in and sat down, you could have heard a pin drop. I looked around the room and no one would look me in the eyes. Everyone just stared at the floor. Finally, Dad told me that they had decided that I should confess to God and the church for having a pistol, and I was to promise to never do it again. Now, there was no way that I was going to say all that, so what I said was, "I'm sorry I owned a pistol," then I got up and looked at the three members that still owned pistols. They just stared at the floor and refused look at me. After that, I walked out without being dismissed and went home. That was my last confession to an Amish audience.

That afternoon when Dad and Mom arrived home from church, Dad didn't say much to me, and I noticed he looked sad and tired. I couldn't help but pity him. After all, he was my father, but I was angry, and I still couldn't figure out why he felt it was necessary to try to make an example out of me. I really felt betrayed, not just by him, but by the whole church. For the next couple of months, Dad and I barley spoke. I began to spend less time at home. To help fill in the gaps, I would go to our non-Amish neighbors some evenings and watch TV. The rest of the time when I wasn't working, I stayed in my room and read western books. At this point I knew that I was leaving the Amish, I just needed a plan.

A few weeks after the Pistol incident, my sister Mary and her husband Dave left the Amish and joined a black-car Mennonite church in Bedford Pa. One evening, I walked to a pay phone and called Dave. I asked him if I could stay with them for a few weeks if I left the Amish. He told me I could. I asked him to please not say anything to anyone and that I would probably be there in a couple of weeks. He promised to keep it quiet and told me to let him know when I was ready. I told him I would.

I knew getting away was one thing, but having a sustainable plan to stay away was not so easy. I knew that I would need three things at a minimum: food, shelter, and a job. The U.S. Military, more specifically, the U.S. Coast Guard, was the one place where I was guaranteed to have all three. I also thought that if I join the Military, then just maybe the Amish wouldn't hound me as much about returning to the church due to my enlistment for four years. That plan could not have worked any better.

During the next few weeks, I put together a plan. I decided to go to N.Y. to visit my cousin Joe and his Wife Mary. I told Dad I wasn't sure how long I would be staying, that way he wouldn't be expecting me to come home at a certain time. After that I hitched a ride to the Liverpool bank where I had my savings account and drew out my entire savings of $1700.00 and closed the account. After that, I went home and packed my suitcase with just a few Amish clothes, a pair of jeans, and a shirt, which I had purchased previously at a thrift store and kept hidden in an old wooden box in the barn. Also in that box was a brand new, shiny replacement social security card. I did not have a birth certificate, but for whatever reason Dad had gotten me a social security card, but he kept it hidden in a safe place, and I didn't know where it was. I knew that if I asked him for it, he would immediately be suspicious and want to know what I wanted it for, so I decided it would be less hassle just to send away for a replacement, which is what I did.

The next day, I said goodbye and walked out of the home that I knew so well, knowing that I would never return there to live, and when I did return to visit, I would be shunned by my family. The gravity of that moment was staggering. Somehow, I was able to maintain my composure even though my emotions were running wild. When I arrived at the bus station, I purchased a one way ticked to N.Y. and climbed aboard. As I sat in my seat, my adrenaline was off the charts. I began to feel a small sense of freedom, even though I had only executed the first part of my plan, but then again, this time it was MY plan. I wasn't depending on anyone else to make my escape. My success rested squarely on my shoulders, and I was comfortable with that. This time I was calling my own shots, and I wouldn't be going back, no matter what.

When I arrived in N.Y., I really had to struggle not to appear too giddy or carefree. After all, as far as Joe and Mary were concerned, I was just there for a short visit, then going back home. I, however, could hardly make myself stay there for even one full week. I felt that I was wasting valuable time, but I also knew that a shorter stay could raise suspicion, and I simply couldn't chance that.

After staying there approximately one week, Joe and Mary gave me a ride to the town of Norwood, where I would catch the bus. I said goodbye to them. Soon after, I boarded the bus to Massena N.Y., where I bought a ticket to Bedford Pa. I also called my brother-in-law Dave from the bus stop to tell him when I would arrive. He agreed to pick me up at the bus stop in Bedford.

After I finished the call to Dave, I slipped into the restroom and changed into my jeans and shirt. Then once again, I ditched my Amish clothes into a trash can, this time for good. As I stepped out of the restroom, I saw that my connecting bus had arrived, so I entered the room where the ticket counter was and headed for the front door, when, there at the counter, stood an Amish man that I knew very well. Luckily, he happened to be looking the other way and didn't notice me. Instantly, my heart started beating out of my chest and my palms were sweating as I dashed back into the other room and out the back door. I was near panic and not thinking straight. I knew I would have to calm down and get on that bus somehow, so I maneuvered in line with the other passengers and walked sideways with my back to the building and my head down until I boarded the bus.

After I found a seat and sat down, I was hit with every emotion known to man. Soon though, I felt a huge weight lift from my shoulders, and I began to feel a real sense of freedom. For the first time in my life, I felt I could finally breath. I didn't feel like I was being suffocated anymore. I was experiencing feelings of sadness and happiness all jumbled together. I can't even describe it.

Later, while riding the bus to Bedford, I had lots of time to think. I thought that, in simple terms, my life began when I was born, however, at this very moment is when I was actually able to start living. A feeling of happiness like I had never felt before began to flow through my veins. I had finally made my break.

CHAPTER

9

Living Begins

It was January 1985, and I felt a little on edge as the greyhound bus passed the city limit sign into Bedford Pa. I was feeling a little sad, thinking about my father and how his heart would be broken when he found out that it was me that had abandoned him this time. Later that evening, I wrote a letter to him, explaining where I was, and that I was safe. I also assured him that my leaving was not his fault, that I simply had chosen a different life, I still loved him with all my heart, and would visit as often as I could. I asked him to please forgive me for the choice I had made for myself.

Finally, when the bus slowed to a stop in front of the station, there along the street was Dave and his oldest daughter Leah, waiting to greet me as I disembarked.

When we arrived at Dave and Mary's house, Mary greeted us at the door and asked me if I was okay. I told her that I was, but that I just couldn't believe that it had finally happened after all these years. She told me to come on in, dinner was on the table. That evening Dave and I talked about my plans and some of the first things that I needed to get done. I told him that I wanted to take my written test for my driving permit as soon as possible. Dave agreed and said he would take me the following Saturday when he didn't have to work.

The following Saturday Dave and I went to the DMV, and I was given a book to study in preparation for the test. Since I didn't have a job, I was able to spend most of the week studying and planning my next moves. I knew that I needed to get two things as soon as possible to advance. One was a driver's license and two a GED. Around the same time that I sent for a replacement social security card, I also sent for a birth certificate. What I got in return was an official-looking paper which read, "THIS IS A, NO RECORD CERTIFICATE, to be used when a birth certificate is required." I had my doubts about it but thought I would give it a try.

The following Saturday, Dave took me back to the DMV, and I took my written test, and to my surprise, I aced it. After they stamped my permit, Dave and I went to a used car lot to look for a car that I could afford. What we found was a 1974 Plymouth duster, marked $800.00. It was eleven years old but looked in decent shape, and it only had 45,000 miles on it, or so we thought. When we asked the salesman if those were original miles, he said, "That's what it says." Dave was a little skeptical, so we offered him $700.00, and he took it. We told the salesman that we would be back the next day to pick it up, and he said that would be okay.

When we got back to the house I began to call around for insurance. I was shocked when the cheapest rate I could find was $1,800 dollars per year. Lucky for me, they agreed to let me pay it in installments. One thing was clear, I needed a job, and soon. My $1,700.00 dollars was disappearing rapidly. The next day Dave asked one of his friends to drive his car home from the lot, and I drove my very own car, with Dave nervously sitting in the passenger seat. Needless to say, he wasn't the only one that was nervous. When we finally arrived at home, I was so tense I could barely get out of the car.

My sister Lydia and her husband George, who had left the Amish earlier, still lived in Snyder Co. Pa., where they owned a cabinet shop about two miles from my dad's place. I needed a job, so I reached out to George and asked him if he would have work for me, just for a little while until I could join the military. He said he did, so we agreed that he would pay me a little for gas and insurance, and the rest would go towards room and board. He then said that in a couple of days he would bring a friend along down to Bedford and pick me up. One of them would drive my car since I didn't have any driving experience yet. I told him that sounded good and that I would see him Wednesday.

Dave had to work Monday and Tuesday, so I practiced driving my car in and out of his lane, which was a couple of hundred feet in length. After a while, I began to get the feel of accelerating and braking, while also learning to relax just a bit.

That following Wednesday evening, it was raining and dark when George and his friend pulled in the lane. After his friend got out of the car, I was surprised to see George turn around and take off for home. I said goodbye to Dave and Mary, took my few belongings out to the passenger side of the car, and opened the door to get in. There sat George's friend in the passenger seat. I was confused to say the least. Who in their right mind would want me to drive, especially on a dark and rainy night like this, and on a major highway for 130 miles? So I asked him if he was going to drive, and he said, "Nope, you're driving." I nervously sat down in the driver's seat. Then, I drove out the road and onto the interstate highway.

What a trip. I was so tense I couldn't even swallow. Big rigs were dogging my rear, some were passing us, all of them were in one heck of a hurry. I didn't have any real concept of maintaining a steady speed, so it seemed like I was going either way too fast or way too slow. In the meantime, the stupid car seemed to have a mind of its own. For some reason I needed to constantly move the steering wheel to stay in my lane, like it was wandering back and forth. To me it seemed like the steering was a bit loose. Finally, I chanced a quick glance at my passenger. His eyes were clenched shut and he was hanging on with both hands. I also noticed that for some weird reason, both his legs appeared to be straight out the front, pushing on the floorboards. I couldn't help but grin a little in the darkness, as I thought, "Serves you right, you stupid nut, you should've taken the wheel when you had the chance." I have no idea how it happened, but somehow, we made it to George's place alive. I barely had the car in park before my passenger was baling out and baling into his own car. I tried to yell thanks as he whizzed by, but for some reason he didn't even look at me. I thought "HUH," he must be late for something. After that, I gathered my things and went into the house. George asked, "How did it go?" I said, "Pretty good, I think your friend slept most of the way, he hardly even opened his eyes." George looked doubtful but didn't say anything more about it.

The following two days, I helped in the cabinet shop, so the only time I could get any practice driving was in the evenings, but only for a short drive. You see, George had just recently been issued his license, so he also wanted to drive. That didn't leave much practice time for me. In the meantime, I started to feel a real sense of urgency regarding my GED, or lack of a GED. I still didn't know what the process was for getting a GED, and I felt that getting my driver's license as soon as possible would give me the freedom that I needed to go to a class if I had to.

The following Saturday, I asked George if he could take me to the driver's license center so I could take my driver's test,. He looked at me and said, "You know, you've only had your permit seven days, are you sure you're ready?" I told him, "The worst that can happen is I'll fail and have to take it again." He agreed. So we went. We ended up taking George's car since it was newer. The downside was I had never driven his car before. It didn't take long for me to notice that for some reason, it was much easier to stay in my lane without wandering all over the place, and I began to wonder if there was something wrong with my car.

After we arrived at the DMV, I got in line with all the other student drivers, mostly kids, and waited for an instructor. I'm not going to lie, I was nervous, and my adrenaline was cooking. To me this was a huge milestone in my life, and I really needed to pass in order to move forward. Eventually, it was my turn. My instructor was a very stern, older, red-haired lady. She glared at me and said let's go, and go we did. I don't remember much about the actual test, but when I finally parked the car and looked at the instructor, I was sure by the stern look she gave me that I must have failed. After glaring at me for what seemed like forever, she said, "You only had your permit for seven days, why are you taking your test so soon?" I gave her my most pitiful look, and said, "You see, I just left the Amish, and I don't have anyone to ride with me." She glared at me for another minute or so, but not quite as sternly I thought. After she let out a long sigh, she uttered some of the sweetest words I had ever heard, "Okay, I will pass you." I could have hugged her but was way too shy for that. After she stamped my permit, I thanked her.

Later that afternoon, I went for a long drive, and eventually I ended up on the road leading to my home place. I had a desire to see my dad and to make sure he was okay. I wasn't sure how it would go, but I knew this was an egg I would have to crack sooner or later, so I decided to get it over with.

After slowly pulling into my dad's driveway, I put my car in park and just sat there for a little while until I was able to work up enough courage to get out. As I began walking toward the house, the front door opened, and Dad came out to greet me. And to my surprise, he wasn't angry, he just looked sad. After we exchanged greetings, he told me to come on in, so I did, and we talked about what the future held for me concerning the Amish church. Dad told me that I would have to be shunned, but he would try to hold off as long as he could, just in case I changed my mind. I told him that I knew I was going to be shunned, and since I had no plans to return, he might as well get it over with. Then he asked what my plans were, and because I still didn't feel comfortable telling him that I wanted to join the Military, I told him that I would try to get a job, then go from there. I was there probably close to an hour when I said goodbye and told him that I would visit again soon. I got back in my car and returned to my sister's place.

I was still being pushed by a strong sense of urgency and a desire to meet all the requirements necessary to enlist, so I called the local high school and asked some lady what I had to do to get my GED. She asked me how many grades I had completed. I told her eight grades in an Amish school. After a long silence, she said I would have to come to the high school and take a pretest so she could determine how many summer schools I would have to attend. I was devastated and told her so. I could not afford to wait several years to follow my dream. She seemed to detect my frustration, because she tried to cheer me up by telling me that I should come in and take the pretest, then we would go from there.

Later that week, I went to the high school and took the test. It wasn't all that hard, except for the Algebra. I had never experienced Algebra in the Amish school, so I had to figure those problems out as best as I could. After the lady checked my answer sheet, she told me that I would have to take one summer school, and that the school wouldn't start for another three months. She then gave me a GED study book and told me to study it to prepare for the school. I wasn't ready to concede to that idea just yet, so I asked her if there was any chance that I would pass if I just took the test. She said, "No, you will fail." "Besides," she said, "the school wouldn't be giving a GED test until after the summer school."

After I got home, I read some of the study book, and it just didn't seem all that hard. I just knew that I could probably pass the test if only I would be allowed to take it. So, the next day, I began calling around to different high schools in the hopes of finding one that would let me test. Finally, after many calls, I finally found a school that said that they were administering a GED test the following week. The lady said that she could register me for it if I would like. I told her, "I would like." Every evening, throughout the rest of the week, I studied my little study book, in anticipation of my upcoming test.

Finally, test day arrived. I was to be there early in the morning because it was a six-hour test. I could barely contain my excitement when they put me in a room by myself and laid the test material in front of me. The lady then told me that I had to stay in the room, except for bathroom breaks, at which time I was to knock on the door, and she would let me out. After a grueling six hours, I was finally done, so I handed my answer sheet to the lady to be checked. I couldn't wait to see if I had passed, so I was a little disappointed when she told me that they would send me the results in about a week.

The next week seemed to go by agonizingly slow, as I eagerly checked the mail every day, waiting for an envelope from the high school. About one week later, on the dot, I opened the mailbox, and there it was. My hands were trembling as I ripped open the envelope and read, *Congratulations, you have passed your GED test.* I thought, so much for summer school.

CHAPTER

10

Pre-enlistment

I found that I was becoming a lot more confident in my abilities every time I was able to beat the odds, such as when I passed my driving test after seven days of practice, and now I had just passed my GED test, basically without studying. I wasn't actually aware of it at the time, but it occurred to me later that I simply wasn't willing to except "no" for an answer. Now that I had all the documents required to enlist (or so I thought), I began to comb through the phone book for a Coast Guard recruiter, but for some reason I simply could not find one. So, I decided to call a Navy recruiter, and maybe he would be able to give me a number. I was a bit naïve at the time, and didn't understand the competitive nature of recruiters, however, I was soon to find out. "Come on in," he said, "I'll go over your paperwork, just to make sure you have every-thing in order, and then, if you still want to join the Coast Guard, I will give you the number." So, I made an appointment with him for later that week.

When I arrived at the Navy recruiter's office, I noticed that there were a ton of very impressive posters of Navy ships hanging all over the wall, and

I began to think, wow, that sure does look exciting. The recruiter seemed friendly enough, I thought, as he asked to see my GED, Driver's license, and birth certificate, which wasn't really a birth certificate, but a no-record-certificate. After studying my documents a while, he slowly looked up at me, and said, "I need to see a real birth certificate." I then told him, "I simply don't have one. My dad delivered me at home and never bothered to get one for me." He then got up and went into another room to consult with his supervisor. Soon he came back and asked if I had any siblings that would remember when and where I was born. I told him there were several that were old enough to remember, so he told me to ask them to write a statement on a piece of tablet paper, saying that they remember my birth and where I was born. They would then have to get them notarized. These statements would then be placed in my military records as proof of birth. Now, getting a statement from my sister Lydia, who had left the Amish, wasn't a problem. Getting one from sister Emma, who was still Amish, posed a slight problem. If she knew that I needed a document to join the Military, she wouldn't have given me one, so I told her it was for a job. After that she agreed to have it ready in a day or two.

A few days later I had both statements, so I returned to the recruiter. After he looked them over, he said, "Good, these will work." He then said that it would take about two weeks to do a background check.

In the meantime, he scheduled a physical and an ASVAB test for me, along with about forty other potential recruits. This would take place in Wilkes-Barre, a town approximately sixty miles north of us. I was to meet a bus nearby, along with other potential recruits, after which we would all take our physicals and ASVAB tests together. He also said that it would likely be an all-day affair, so I shouldn't expect to be home until after dark that evening.

I will admit, the following couple of days were a little nerve-racking. I really didn't know what a physical was. I had never had a physical before, so I didn't know what to expect. All I knew was that it was something that had to be done to join the Military, and it gave me some comfort knowing that everyone was getting the same treatment, something I wasn't used to.

The day finally came to meet the bus. The ride to Wilkes-Barre seemed to take a long time. No one spoke, everyone seemed to be in deep thought, and I suppose, apprehensive. Soon after we arrived, we were lined up in single file and told not to talk unless we were spoken to by one of the staff. I wasn't much for talking anyway, so that suited me just fine. Basically, I didn't know what I was doing, so I just did what everyone else was doing and hoped no one would notice. After a while, the day turned into a blur. We were poked and prodded, we lifted weights, we were weighed and measured, then we were lined up single file in a massive room and told to undress, except for our skivvies. Now, for a young Amish lad who wasn't even allowed to take his shirt off in public not more than a few weeks ago, this was a culture shock. Then it got even worse. As the doctor moved down the line, he had each one of us drop our skivvies, while he checked out every inch of our bodies. When he was finished, I felt, I could handle anything they could throw at me. I took a quick glance down the line and saw that I wasn't the only one that was embarrassed, which made me feel a little better about myself.

Later that day, we were all given our ASVAB tests. I had trouble keeping my mind on the test, especially after all I had been through that day. I did, however, manage to finish in the allotted time. Some time later, some of the staff brought us our results. They took each one of us in person and told us what our scores were. After that, we were allowed to pick what job we wanted as long as it fell within the parameters of our score, sort of a job placement exercise, if you will. Soon it was my turn. A Navy Petty Officer asked me to sit down at his desk, then he told me that I had missed the required score to enlist into the active duty Navy by just one point, but that I qualified to join the Navy reserve, and he would be happy to help me pick a job if I wanted to do that. I was devastated, I needed a full-time job, not the part-time job that the reserves would be, and I told him so. He then told me that the Navy was getting more recruits than it needed, so they raised the score requirements in order to slow it down. He also said that the other three branches hadn't raised their scores yet, so I might be able to enlist in one of them, if I was interested. I then asked him if he knew of a Coast Guard recruiter, because that is what I wanted to join in the first place. He hesitated for a moment, then said,

"Come with me," so I followed him down the hall and through a doorway. Above the door were the words I had been longing for: U.S. Coast Guard. As we entered the room, I saw many posters on the wall, and on those posters were photos of the most beautiful boats I had ever seen. On each boat was painted in large letters, "U.S. Coast Guard." At that moment, I knew that I had found my home.

The Navy Petty Officer told me to wait by the door while he spoke to a man sitting behind a desk. This man had on a very sharp looking blue uniform, but the most outstanding feature was his beard, (back then the Coast Guard still allowed men to grow beards). After they finished talking, the Coast Guard recruiter motioned for me to approach his desk. He then asked me where I was from. I told him, and he then told me that he couldn't recruit me because I wasn't from his area, but that he knew a recruiter in Harrisburg, and he would give him a message to call me as soon as he could. After thanking him, I went back out to the waiting room until the bus came to take us home.

After a few anxious days, my sister came out into the cabinet shop where I was working and told me that a Coast Guard recruiter was on the phone, waiting to talk to me. I dropped everything and ran to answer the phone. I said "hello," and a man on the other end of the line introduced himself as Petty officer so and so with the U.S. Coast Guard. After he asked me a few questions, he said he would like me to come to his office, and that he had a few more questions for me. He also said he had a video that he was required to show me concerning boot camp, so that I would know what to expect.

I asked him when he would like me to come in. He said the next day would be fine, so I told him I would see him then. The following day, I drove to Harrisburg and met him at his office, where he asked me about my drug use. I told him that I had never used any. After that he had me watch a video about basic training, which consisted of a lot of yelling in your face, and lots of physical training, then at the end it showed graduation. He then asked if I was willing to endure a life like that for eight weeks. I assured him I could hardly wait. He told me that he was able to use the Navy physical but would have to do his own background investigation, which would take about two weeks. He said that after I passed, he would give me a date to come in again, and at that time, I would be sworn in and shipped to Cape May N.J. for eight weeks of basic training. I had a hard time believing that my dream was actually about to come true. Less than three months ago, I was still a member of the Old Order Amish church with very little hope of ever getting out. Now look at me. I couldn't help but think of the guys at my old welding shop that told my brothers, "He'll be back, there's no way, he'll make it in the real world."

Meanwhile, my old car was still having trouble staying between the lines. The steering seemed to have excessive wear, so I took it to a garage to have it looked at. After checking it out, the mechanic asked me how many miles it had on it. I told him the odometer said 45,000. He laughed and said, "More like 145,000." He said the ball joints were worn out, and that it really wasn't even safe to drive in that condition.

He also said that it would cost a lot to fix. Well, I didn't have that kind of money, so I decided to think about it a while. On the way home from the garage, I stopped at a car wash to try and clean it up a bit, and when I hit it with the pressure washer, to my surprise the entire rear fender disappeared. I could have bawled. I haven't seen that much rust and Bondo on a single vehicle before or since. After I got home, I asked George what he thought I should do. He said that we should look for a better used car, so we went to a local dealer, the same place George bought his car. There we found a 1979 Chrysler, LeBaron, bright red with a red interior. I mean it was just plain red, but I couldn't afford to be picky. The price was 3.000.00. I didn't have near enough money, so I would have to apply for a loan. Somehow, George was able to shame the dealer into taking my old car in on trade. He balked and carried on, but in the end, he gave in, making my new car a little more affordable. George was nice enough to offer to make my payments for me while I was in Boot Camp. He said I could pay him back after I graduated, which I did.

The day before I was to report to my recruiter, I went to see my dad to tell him that I was enlisting in the Coast Guard, and that I wouldn't be able to come see him for at least eight weeks. I had no idea how this visit would go, but I felt I owed it to him. To be truthful, when I went in the house, he was sitting in his old rocking chair (the same one that he sat in to rock me to sleep when I was a baby). I now have that rocking chair in my house. We exchanged greetings, then I told him that I was enlisting the next day. He didn't seem very surprised at all. In fact he seemed to look relieved. He asked me what I would be doing when I graduated. I told him that our primary mission was search and rescue, and law enforcement. We talked a while longer, than we said goodbye, and I drove to my sister's place to pack for the next day. That night I didn't get much sleep.

April 22nd, 1985, just three and a half months after leaving the Old Order Amish. With just a few dollars and a dream, I found myself standing in front of my recruiter, right hand raised, repeating after him, "I, Simon Troyer, swear to defend and protect the constitution of the United States, from all enemies, both foreign and domestic, and to obey all lawful orders given to me by my superiors, so help me God." I was swelling with pride as I boarded a bus, enroute to Cape May N.J. and eight weeks of Boot Camp.

CHAPTER

11

Boot Camp

It was late evening, the sun was almost set, when the Greyhound bus rolled to a stop in front of the station in Cape May, New Jersey. During the ride, I met a few other recruits that were also going to the same Boot Camp I was going to. As we got off the bus, we met even more recruits. All of us were headed to the same place. We had all been instructed to wait at the bus station, that someone from the Coast Guard base would come pick us up in a school bus. We still had some time, so I decided to use the bathroom, and to my surprise, there were several recruits desperately smoking Marijuana for the last time. They offered some to me, which I declined. I had never used Pot, nor did I have any intentions to ever use Pot. I literally couldn't understand why they were willing to take such a risk at being expelled from Boot Camp. I had simply worked too hard to finally get here, and I wasn't willing to take any chances, so I went back out to the street to watch for the bus.

Around ten PM, the bus finally arrived. By now I was beginning to get tired. It had been a long day so far, and the night before I had slept very little in anticipation of what today would hold. So, by now, I was looking forward to getting to the base and getting a good night's sleep.

The bus driver was a low-ranking Petty Officer, assigned to driving the Recruit bus, not a gold medal job by Military standards. He lazily opened the door, then, rather un-enthusiastically told us to get on. I was ready to get this camp started, so I was the first one on board. Some of the recruits took their good old time meandering up the steps and into a seat. Soon we were headed for the base. On the way, there were many questions asked of the driver, mostly on what to expect when we got there. He informed us that if we just look at Boot Camp as a mind game, and don't take anything personal, we would be fine.

When we approached the main gate, a man wearing white gloves waved the bus on through. I couldn't help but notice, as we passed under the street-lights, that half the recruits appeared to be sound asleep. I marveled at that, because I was way too excited to be sleepy anymore. It had just dawned on me that I was actually at Boot Camp, and my dream was no longer just a dream. Following a short drive onto the base, the bus rolled to a stop beside what appeared to be a dimly lit parking lot. There I saw three men standing in the dim light, all three were wearing Stetson hats, better known as smoky bear hats. I also saw a bunch of little yellow footprints painted on the mac-adam, and I wondered what they were for.

Basic training, better known as Boot camp, is not where some overzealous Company Commanders get their jollies, giving a bunch of young Recruits a hard time. It has a valuable purpose. Without it, the military would consist of a bunch of self-centered individuals concerned only about their own personal needs and desires. A military like that would of course be worthless. Instead, the idea of Boot Camp is to take a bunch of spoiled, rotten, self-centered individuals, and break them down by applying a combination of stress, sleep deprivation, mental, and physical fatigue. After that, the individuals will be molded into a team of well-trained, fighting men and women. They will have been trained in the basic military skills, such as small arms training and how to escape and evade if captured by the enemy. Also they will have learned to work as a cohesive team, caring for each other, because they may have to depend on each other for survival. They will learn to follow orders without hesitation, where one second could mean the difference between life and death. And so, it began.

I began to wonder why we were allowed to sit there in the darkness for such a long time. It seemed almost intentional, almost like someone wanted us to fall asleep. Whatever it was, it seemed to be working. I glanced away from the three men just long enough to take a quick look around the bus. Sure enough, most of the recruits were sound asleep. Not me. I could feel the electric in the air. I was sure something exciting was about to happen.

After a while, I saw one of the three men position himself at the front of the painted footprints. He then straightened his uniform and adjusted his Stetson a little lower on his forehead. The other two men also fussed with their uniforms as they approached the door of the bus, which, at this time, was still closed. It was around 11:30 pm when one of the men gave the driver a hand signal, at which time the driver opened the door very quietly. I watched with apprehension as I saw the top of a Stetson easing up the steps of the bus. One second later, my world as I knew it was over; the brightest lights I had ever seen inside a bus were turned on. At the same time, a metal trash can was kicked down the aisle, followed by a very intimidating, very large Company Commander, screaming at the top of his lungs. "WHAT ARE YOU PEOPLE STILL DOING ON MY BUS? AND HOW DARE YOU SHOW UP AT MY BOOT CAMP AND SLEEP? WHO GAVE YOU PERMISSION TO SLEEP? GRAB YOUR BAGS AND GET OFF MY BUS NOW, YOU HAVE TWO SECONDS, ONE, TWO." Then it started all over again, because of course some hadn't made it off in his time frame. I slipped by him when his back was turned and headed for the door.

As we bailed out the door, the other company commander, positioned outside the door of the bus lit into us with a tirade of his own. "WHO GAVE YOU PEOPLE PERMISSION TO WALK? I WANT TO SEE YOU RUNNING, YOU ARE THE SORRIEST BUNCH OF MOMMA BABIES I'VE EVER SEEN, WHAT WERE THOSE STUPID RECRUITERS THINKING SENDING YOU TO MY BOOTCAMP. NONE OF YOU

WILL GRADUATE UNLESS YOU LEARN TO FOLLOW ORDERS, NOW GET ON YOUR FOOTPRINTS."

And so, we ran. After we all found a set of footprints to stand on, I began to see the purpose of it all. It was placing us in perfect formation. The yelling and screaming didn't stop there. Recruits started to set their bags down, and it was like the CC's were expecting it, and were waiting for it. "WHO GAVE YOU PERMISSION TO SET YOUR BAG DOWN? NOW PICK THAT BAG UP OVER YOUR HEAD AND GIVE ME TEN JUMPING JACKS.

Then it was my turn. "YOU, WHY AREN'T YOU STANDING AT ATTENTION?

"I DON'T KNOW HOW SIR," I yelled.

"HOW DARE YOU TALK TO ME LIKE THAT? YOU WILL BEGIN YOUR SENTENCE WITH SIR, AND END WITH SIR."

"SIR I DON'T KNOW HOW SIR."

"DID YOU JUST MAKE A FACE AT ME?"

Apparently, I grimaced, a no-no in the Military. Facial expressions and outward emotions are not allowed.

"GET IN THE PUSH-UP POSITION, NOW."

I wasn't sure what he meant. I thought I knew how to do a push-up though, so I dropped to a prone position. He was not impressed. Apparently, a push-up position is arms fully extended, holding your body weight above the ground, for as long as he wished.

"DID I GIVE YOU PERMISSION TO LAY DOWN? ARE YOU REALLY THAT DUMB? I HAVE HALF A MIND TO SEND YOU BACK TO YOUR MOMMY AND DADDY. NOW GET UP AND STAND AT ATTENTION."

"SIR, YES SIR."

After that, he moved on to another recruit, and I heard it start all over again.

At first, I felt singled out, but after a while I began to understand that the CC's were, in all fairness, equal opportunity abusers. Before long I felt a little left out when they weren't in my face. After all, this was Boot Camp, and I was thrilled to be here.

After about an hour of screaming and yelling, we were able to reach some semblance of order, at least we looked like we were standing at attention. Two of the CC's kept circling us, looking for anyone who might have the audacity to relax a bit. Some of the recruits were actually really dumb and had to be brought back into line regularly. In the meantime, the other CC was lecturing us on the rules we were expected to follow—eyes in the boat, a term we became intimately familiar with. While standing at attention, we were never to focus our eyes on the face of a senior person, we were to focus over their head, and since we were low-ranking Seaman Recruits, everyone on the base outranked us. We were expected to run everywhere we went, unless we had a medical excuse, or were in formation. When we weren't running or marching, we were to stand at attention or at parade rest, depending on what command was given. When addressing a senior person, or being addressed by a senior person, we were to begin with Sir or Ma'am, and end with Sir or Ma'am. There were lots of do's and don'ts that I won't bore you with, but you get the idea.

It was sometime after midnight when we apparently got it together enough on our footprints that the CC's decided to advance to the next stage of checking in. We were told to follow each other in single file to a nearby building. As we entered the building, I saw what reminded me of several rows of little horse stalls with sort of a shelf about waist high along the fronts of them. We were told to line up in these stalls, one person to a stall. As we began lining up in front of the stalls, some of the recruits began to set their bags on the floor. This started a whole new tirade from the CC's. "WHO TOLD YOU TO SET YOUR BAG DOWN? ARE YOU LAZY OR WHAT? PICK UP THAT BAG UNTILL YOU'RE TOLD TO SET IT DOWN."

Several minutes after we were all in position, still holding our bags, the base commander came in and spoke to us for a while. He welcomed us, then he gave us a quick rundown of what to expect for the next eight weeks. He made it clear that some of us would not be graduating due to attitude or perhaps medical issues, etc. After he left the room, another person took his place at the podium and finally told us to empty our bags on the little shelf. After that we were allowed to set our empty bags down. Then he went through a list of things we couldn't have. Anything we couldn't have, we were to throw into a garbage can. I ended up throwing about half of my belongings away, it seemed.

Around 1:30ish in the morning, we were marched outside and placed in formation again, then, marched (more like walked; we didn't know how to march yet) to our barracks, where we would spend the next two months of our lives. By the time we were assigned a bunk, either the top one or, if you were lucky, the bottom one (I was lucky), it was after 2:00 AM, and we were totally exhausted. We were asleep soon after lying down.

It seemed like I had just fallen asleep when I began to hear a faint click-ing sound in my dream. The sound started to get louder and louder until it resembled someone walking. It sounded a lot like a horse with a loose shoe, walking on the blacktop (actually it was a metal plate attached to the bottom of a shoe. These were normally worn by the honor guard, but at the time I had no idea). The clicking stopped right outside our door. By now, I was semi-awake and expecting something. Suddenly the door flew open, the bright lights came on, and a metal trash can came clattering down the hall, followed by a screaming CC: "WHAT ARE YOU DOING STILL SLEEPING? GET UP, YOU HAVE FIVE SECONDS TO BE AT ATTENTION, IN FRONT OF YOUR RACK." It was 0300 in the morning. I couldn't believe how fast forty guys could get up and get to attention. One young man literally fell from the top bunk to the floor. He was discharged with a broken leg. That's when some of the less serious recruits began to realize that this wasn't summer camp, and if you wanted to graduate you had better shape up.

That day we learned that if you weren't at the head of the line for chow, you literally had five minutes to eat, and it didn't matter if you were fin-ished or not. That first morning, we received our shaved heads and our uniforms, then we were assigned to a company. Ours was company-Q, pro-nounced K-BECK.

We received many instructions that day. Everything was starting to become a blur. I wasn't prepared for what followed. We had to line up in single file and walk through this building. Someone said we were getting our inoculations. I barely even knew what that meant, but I was about to find out. As we moved ahead in single file, I saw people in white coats standing in a line with five-gallon buckets in front of them. Out of these buckets came a small hose with a sprayer nozzle looking thing attached to the end. As I moved closer I could see the person in the white coat hold the nozzle against the arm of a recruit. This was followed by a command not to move. After that, I heard a sound like a small caliber rifle being discharged, generally followed by a moan from the recruit. To say I was uneasy would be an understatement, but when I saw that it didn't straight up kill anyone, I manned up and took my turn. Wow, that hurt. Never in a million years would I have guessed that you could give someone a shot with air pressure instead of a needle.

After the first couple of days, when all the check-ins were done, we finally met our very own CC. He was a big husky Chief Boatswains Mate with a gravelly voice, not much for talking, but when he spoke, you knew you had better pay attention, and for some unknown reason I liked him right from the start.

I really don't remember much about the first week. It was such an extreme adjustment, especially for a young Amish boy like me, everything we did was totally new to me. Take calisthenics for instance. I thought I knew how to do sit-ups and push-up, but apparently not the right way, so I had to learn how to do them all over again. Not to mention jumping jacks. I'd never even heard of such a thing.

I would try my best to watch what the other recruits did, then follow suit. This worked most of the time, but sometimes I would get called out for it. We had to learn how to salute, how to march, left and right o-bleaks, about face, squaring our corners, standing at attention, standing at ease, and always with our eyes in the boat.

We were issued laundry bags early on. We had to write our name and company on them, then, once a week they would be picked up and taken to a large washing machine where the entire bag full of laundry would be tossed in. In other words, the laundry would never leave the bag. It was dried the same way, then returned to us. You can imagine how wrinkled our clothes were when we finally took them out of the bags. We had to iron and mend our own clothes, and not one wrinkle was allowed. We took our showers in the evening in a large shower room, ten of us at a time. We quickly learned how to manage our time. Between swim training, marching, and academics in class, along with dental appointments and medical appointments, there wasn't a spare second left at the end of the day.

After a few days, I noticed that some of the recruits were beginning to form their own little groups. Up until now, I tried to keep a low profile, so I didn't really fit into any group. Mainly I kept myself busy ironing my uniforms and getting ready for the next day. This worked for a while until one day the California group noticed that I wasn't playing along with their stupid little game of Name That Tune. One of them would mimic a movie soundtrack, and the rest of the group would try to guess what movie it belonged to.

Meanwhile, I was quietly minding my own business when one of them decided to ask me why I wasn't getting involved in their game. I didn't know what to say, so I just told them that I didn't really know any soundtracks. That prompted one of them to jokingly ask, "Why not, were you Amish, or what?" You could have heard a pin drop when I said, "Yes, up until three months ago." I was immediately bombarded with the usual questions from some; others didn't seem too surprised, and I began to feel relieved that now it was out. Now I could deal with the aftermath. Everyone seemed to be okay with it, except the California boys.

I noticed right away that they seemed to avoid me. I would see them whisper to each other, then, they would glance my way. They just didn't seem comfortable around me. Finally, one of them worked up the nerve to ask me, "Is it true the Amish only shower once a week?" I jokingly told them that most Amish don't even have showers.

A few days went by, when, to my surprise, I was summoned to the CC's office. I had no idea why, so I was a little taken aback when the CC asked me if I shower regularly. I told him I shower every day with the rest of the recruits. He then informed me that some of the recruits complained that I had body odor, and, he reminded me, that if I didn't get it under control, I could be kicked out for it. I said, "Sir, yes Sir" and returned to our barracks.

When I opened the door to the barracks, the California boys were all sitting there watching me enter, snickering and laughing. I walked right passed them like nothing was going on, all the while thinking to myself, *Ok fellas, game on.* They were going to regret trying to get me kicked out. I should probably have planned it a little better, because a few days later, when I made my move, I almost got myself kicked out.

Boot camp was filled with deadlines and timelines. We were tested on everything. We were allowed to have one failure per test, but you had better pass on the second attempt or you could be reverted back two weeks to the company behind you, resulting in a ten-week boot camp instead of eight weeks. We made every attempt to avoid being reverted, although it wasn't terribly uncommon.

One of the requirements, was earning your green belt within the first two weeks. The way you earned it was perfecting your facing movements, along with learning the phonetic alphabet and many other things by heart. When you thought you knew everything sufficiently, you would report to the CC's office, where you would stand at attention, with your eyes in the boat and answer any questions he might ask you. During this episode, most recruits, including myself, were extremely nervous. The humiliation of failing sucked, so you tried hard to keep it together. If you were successful, the CC would hand you a green belt to wear around your waist. This was the first boost of confidence we could earn in basic training. It brought us a little respect for the first time since arriving, and the belt was coveted by all.

I had been studying hard for my belt and had almost worked up enough courage to give it a try. Now the California boys had already earned their belts along with about half of the other recruits, yet every time a recruit would go to the CC's office to try for his belt, one of the California boys would follow him up to the CC's door. After a while, he would return to his cronies and report all the mistakes that were made. Then, they would all laugh and make fun of the recruit when he returned. This made all of us a lot more nervous, knowing that any mistake we made would be broadcast to the rest of the recruits.

I decided that something had to be done about it. Here is where I almost made a fatal mistake. The next recruit that went out into the hallway to try for his belt was predictably followed by the California ringleader. He in turn was followed by me. My thought was that when he was hiding outside the

CC's door, collecting information, I would give him a slight nudge, causing him to step into the doorway. My hope was, that the CC would see him and question what he was doing outside the barracks, since he already had his green belt. I hoped this would put a stop to him following every recruit out into the hall. So, after thinking over my plan for at least a second, I nudged him. After that, my world fell apart.

Unbeknownst to me, a CC, more specifically, the CC with the clicking heels, was standing at the top of the stairs on the second floor, watching our every move. And to him, it probably looked like I had just assaulted an innocent recruit. At any rate, he began screaming as he came running down the steps to our level. He ordered me up against the wall at attention, all the while screaming something about fighting. He then ordered me to return to my bunk and throw all my belongings into my duffle bag. After that, he marched me over to a barracks called discharge hold. He practically threw me in the door and told me to stay there until I was discharged. All this time he never stopped screaming. Every time I tried to speak, he screamed even louder. This all happened in the span of about five minutes. I found a bunk and threw my bag on it. I was heartbroken. I'm not ashamed to admit it. I cried most of the night.

The following morning, I walked to breakfast with all the other recruits, waiting to be discharged. I couldn't eat, I felt like a lost soul, and I couldn't believe my world and dream was over. I had no idea what I would do next, I had a very hard time controlling my emotions, but, somehow, somewhere, deep inside, I held onto a glimmer of hope. I felt that if I could only tell my side of the story, maybe they would let me stay. I held onto that hope as I returned to Discharge Hold and waited for my fate.

Sometime during that forenoon, the door to the barracks burst open, and there stood the CC with the clicking heels. I heard him yell "Seaman recruit Troyer, front and center." I hurried over and stood at attention in front of him. After glaring at me for some time, he told me to report to the CC's office, ASAP. He then turned and clicked away.

A million thoughts raced through my mind as I ran over to my original Barracks, then down the hall to my CC's office. When I arrived in front of his office, the door was closed, so I took a moment to straighten my uniform, then I tentatively knocked on the door, but only one time. I heard someone say "Enter." I opened the door and stood at attention, while I reported like we were taught. "Seaman recruit Troyer, reporting as ordered."

After that, my CC, in a rather calm voice said, "At ease, close the door and have a seat." It was then I noticed there were three CC's sitting in the room. All of them looked relatively friendly, which helped put me at ease.

After I sat down, my CC looked me over for a while, then asked, "Why were you fighting?" I told him that my intention wasn't to fight. He then asked me why I pushed a recruit, so I told him the whole story, how I just wanted to draw his attention to the recruit because he and his cronies made fun of everyone that made mistakes, while trying for their green belts, and that I didn't think it was the right thing to do. He had no real expression on his face, he just looked at me. After a while, one of the other CC's, after shuffling through some papers, said, "Your record states that you were Old order Amish, is that true?" I said, "Sir, yes Sir".

There was a silence that lasted for a few seconds, then the usual questions began. How was it growing up Amish? Did you drive a horse and buggy? What made you leave and join the Coast Guard? Is it true that your family shuns you now? Finally my CC asked me what it meant to me, being in the Coast Guard. I told him that it meant everything to me. He then asked what I would do if they didn't let me stay? At that point, I couldn't help myself. Tears began to trickle down my face as I blubbered these words, "I don't know, I have nowhere else to go."

This was followed by a long silence, as I attempted to compose myself. Finally, my CC told me to go back to Discharge hold, while they decided what to do. I stood up, did an about face, then walked through the door. As I ran back to the Discharge Barracks, my world seemed just a little brighter. No matter what they decided, I felt better, having had the opportunity to tell my side of the story.

CHAPTER
12

Vindication/Graduation

Growing up Amish, of course, meant there was zero tolerance for violence. Now violence to me meant beating someone with your fist or perhaps a wagon spoke. The word assault meant the same thing to me as violence. Blame it on the fact that English was, after all, my third language, and maybe that is why I didn't understand the true definition of assault. Had I known that giving a person a slight nudge would be considered assault, I probably would not have committed such a crime. During the aftermath of the alleged assault, my CC took the opportunity to explain to me the definition of assault. I am grateful to him for taking the time, and to make sure that I understood what assault meant, and that it was not tolerated in the military, except against the enemy, so I governed myself accordingly from that moment forward.

After leaving the CC's office and feeling just a little better, having been given the opportunity to share my reasons for assaulting a fellow recruit, I spent some time sitting on my rack, thinking about what my choices were. If

I should happen to get kicked out, I simply could not come up with a plan. It dawned on me that I had never even considered failure, and I still refused to except it, so it was with that mindset that I sat there on my rack and awaited judgement.

After what seemed like an eternity (only a few hours), the door once again burst open and a CC entered. This time, it was one of the CC's that had been in the office during my previous meeting. He ordered me front and center, then told me to report to the CC's office ASAP. My mind was racing as I ran to the CC's office, once again. Suddenly, I noticed that I was fast overtaking the CC, walking down the same sidewalk. Crap! What was it that I was supposed to say before overtaking and passing a senior person? Oh, yes, so I yelled, "Sir, by your leave Sir." He replied, "Carry on," at that point, I ran by him and arrived at the building.

When I entered the barracks and started down the hallway toward the CC's office, I saw a recruit doing pushups while counting out loud. I couldn't help but notice the clicking-heeled CC leaning over, screaming at him to keep going. I wasn't sure what to do because the recruit was doing his push-ups in the open doorway to the CC's office. I decided I would have to do my report in spite of all this ruckus, because I wasn't told not to. I approached the door and knocked once. My CC looked up and said enter. Now in order for me to enter, I had to step over the recruit, so the screaming CC ordered him to stop doing push-ups. I couldn't resist looking down at him. As I stepped over his prone body, imagine my surprise when I saw the California fun-maker looking up at me with an imploring look on his face.

After I was inside the room, I made my report in the required manner. The CC, without looking up, replied "at ease," so I stood in the (at ease) position for at least five minutes. Meanwhile, the push-ups continued until the recruit was past exhaustion. After that, he switched to leg lifts, then to jumping jacks, then back to push-ups. When the recruit had reached complete muscle failure and couldn't do anything but lay there on the floor, I heard the CC scream, "You like to make fun of people, why don't you make fun of me?" The reply from the recruit, was a very weak, "Sir, no Sir." He then ordered him to attention, and I heard him scream at the recruit to pack his duffle bag.

He was being reverted two weeks. I heard him wobble down the hallway, and suddenly it became very quiet.

A few seconds later, my CC looked at me and said, "Troyer, we decided to let you continue, however, just one more infraction of that nature will get you a ticket home." I said, "Sir, thank you Sir." He then told me to go get my things and return to my barracks. I said, "Sir, yes Sir." I did an about face and ran to get my duffel bag.

Some time after graduation, one of the CC's informed me that had I pushed that recruit strictly for my own benefit, they would not have been so lenient with me, but because I had acted on behalf of the others, they found a degree of loyalty in my actions, and they found that to be commendable. Either way, I felt vindicated.

I knew that I had been given a huge break, and I did not take it for granted. I also knew I would have to survive the remaining six weeks without incident. I realized that I needed to learn as fast as possible how not to think like an Amishman, but to learn the ways of the real world, by watching others and asking questions. I developed a willingness to learn, and to change my life, to try to fit in. in the meantime I aligned myself with the hardest working recruits, I observed and learned from them, I watched how they handled different situations, then I followed suit. I accepted the fact that I had no experiences outside of being Amish, so I had nowhere to go but up.

With this mindset, I attacked the last six weeks of boot camp. Sure I had many challenges, I got close to failing some tests, I was screamed at, I had to do extra calisthenics for screwing up, but the CC's recognized that failure wasn't one of my options. I never asked for any leniency or favors, and none were given. However, there were occasions when the CC would utter words of encouragement to me, when it would go unnoticed by the other recruits. I got the feeling they wanted me to succeed, and that alone gave me the heart to press on.

Finally, we entered the eighth week. By now, K-beck company was operating like a well-oiled machine. Our facing movements, salutes, and marching had become a part of us. Those of us who had stuck it out had by now become adapted to the military life and its traditions. I found that it suited me perfectly. It was like my new family. I couldn't get enough of it.

As was customary, during the eighth week, the top ten graduates were allowed to get first pick where they wanted to be stationed. I wasn't in the top ten, but I wasn't in the bottom ten either. I was somewhere in between, so I wasn't allowed to pick where I wanted to be stationed. There was a saving grace, available to an additional ten recruits though. If they volunteered to work in the warehouse for two weeks after graduation, they would be able to pick their stations from the following companies list. Before they did, I volunteered along with nine others.

Eight weeks after arriving at boot camp, graduation day had finally arrived. It was a bright, sunny, midsummer day. K-beck company, dressed in their dress blues, stood in formation at the front of the line, followed by all the other companies, lined up according to seniority. Everyone was standing at ease to give the dignitaries and the families of the recruits enough time to get seated on the bleachers. The order was then given for attention, followed by MARCH, and march we did. This was our chance to put into practice what we were trained to do. Finally, when we were even with the dignitaries, we were ordered to, Mark time, this was where we marched in place for about three steps, then HALT, after that, at attention, then right face, now we were facing the dignitaries, in unison, we rendered a sharp salute, while the National Anthem, was played. As soon as it was finished playing, we were ordered to the at ease position, while the dignitaries took turns speaking and congratulating us. This only lasted for a few minutes, then back to attention. After that, the CC said, "K-beck company, FALL OUT." That was our cue to throw our caps in the air and whoop and holler, as the families descended off the bleachers to meet their youngsters and celebrate with them.

I did not throw my hat into the air. I was afraid that if I failed to catch it, it might get dirty. I also knew that none of my family would be there. So, I stood on that parade field and reflected over the past eight weeks. I suddenly realized the importance of what had just happened. I remembered that a little over five months ago, I was still Amish, and all this was just a dream. I also remembered the nay-sayers that told my brother, "He'll be back, he won't be able to handle the real world." Well, this was the real world, and I had just conquered the most important hurdle of my life. This graduation would open all the other doors for me. I was now a bona fide, genuine member of the United States Military. My heart was soaring, and I could not have been more proud.

Coast Guard, Graduation

After graduation, we were granted liberty for the weekend. That is, those of us that had volunteered to stay two more weeks. But we first had to move our things to a permanent barracks. These were much nicer than the recruit barracks. We were only two men to a room, and we had our own bathroom. The majority of the other graduates took a few days of leave to spend time with families before reporting to their duty stations or ships.

During boot camp, we were all ranked as Seaman recruits, however, after graduation we were all promoted to Seaman Apprentices. Our uniforms were starting to look better as well. We now all had two stripes on our sleeve. We also had at least one ribbon for graduating. Some had more, depending on how well they shot during weapons training. I had three ribbons, one for graduating, one for shooting expert with the M-16 rifle, and one for shooting expert with the 1911, 45 cal. Pistol. For this, I give credit to all those years of hunting Squirrels along those Pa. ridges using only a single shot .22 cal. Rifle.

I was incredibly excited about starting work in the clothing warehouse. It meant a lot to me, because it meant that all the bootcamp stuff was behind me and now I could start doing real work, and I felt fairly confident in my ability to pick up on things. I also knew that I could ask questions without being screamed at. All of this was giving me confidence. So, with that mind-set, I arrived at the warehouse, at 0700 on Monday morning, ready for duty.

The other nine volunteers and I were met by a Petty officer, who appeared friendly and above all, he talked to us in a normal voice. He told us that the clothing warehouse received uniform orders from all the Coast Guard stations around the country. He stressed the importance of making sure each order was fulfilled exactly as requested. We were told to pay close attention to detail. Our job was to take an order and collect everything listed on it, then stack the items on a counter with the order on top. A Petty officer would then double check the order and approve or disapprove it. After that, someone else would package it for shipment. I really enjoyed my work.

When lunch time rolled around, we were given an entire hour to eat. We no longer ate with the recruits, but with all the regular Coasties. In no time at all, the first week was coming to a close. We would all have two days of liberty for the first time. I overheard some of my cohorts asking if anyone had a car. No one did, so they asked me. I told them that I had one at home, and that I was planning to fly home that weekend, then drive it back down, and be back by Sunday eve. It was only about a five-hour drive. We were all excited about having a car available so we could go to the boardwalk, evenings after work.

That Friday evening, after work, I hired a cab to take me to the airport, where I bought a ticket to Harrisburg, Pa. The plane had about thirteen seats and was filled with cigarette smoke (this was 1985, and there were fewer regulations). This being my first flight, I didn't quite know what to expect, but once we were airborne, I began to enjoy it a lot.

Before I left N.J. I had called a friend to pick me up in Harrisburg. He was waiting when I got there. I didn't have a lot of time to visit with anyone, but I did go see my dad and step-mother. Dad and I were happy to see each other. Even though we had written each other during boot camp, we still had a lot of catching up to do. It surprised me how interested he was about what my job was going to be, and where I would be stationed. I told him I still wasn't sure where I would be going, but I would try to stay within driving distance from him, so I could come visit him sometimes. He seemed pleased with that, so I said goodbye to them and started back to Cape May.

It was Sunday afternoon when I arrived at the base. Some of the guys wanted to go to the boardwalk, so we loaded up and went. The ocean, along with the beach and boardwalk, were all new to me, and I must say for a young Amish lad, the scenery was quite enjoyable as well. I drank an adult beverage while walking the boardwalk and contemplated what my future might hold. I felt at peace. Everything was falling in place just the way I had envisioned. I knew I would face hurdles and obstacles in my future, but I wasn't afraid; I felt that I had the confidence to be successful in whatever came my way.

The following week, we were able to choose our stations. We were given a list of stations with openings. The one that caught my interest was Station Fairport on Lake Erie. It was a small boat station, located about thirty miles east of Cleveland, only a six-hour drive from my dad's house. I was pleased to find one so close to him, so I chose it. I also requested ten days of leave before reporting for duty. By midweek, received my orders, and so did the others. Two of my buddies drew orders for a Cutter based in Connecticut. One of them asked me if I would be willing to drive them home to Connecticut, then cut over to Pa. from there. I had never been to Connecticut, and I loved to drive, so I agreed to do it. If I had known the amount of traffic we would encounter, not to mention driving through the heart of New York city, I would not have offered. Fortunately, the trip ended in Connecticut without incident.

When we arrived at the home of one of the guys, his mother informed us that she had planned a welcome home party for him, and that I was welcome to stay for the night. I felt a little out of place, but with some encouragement, I agreed. That evening a couple dozen young folks arrived and began to party. I'm telling you, to date, I had not experienced anything like this, and I began to get very uncomfortable when some of them began passing around a joint (marijuana). When they finally convinced my so-called buddy to take a hit, I walked backwards towards my car until I felt the door handle. I slid behind the wheel and hit the bricks toward Pa. In those days, we didn't have cell phones or GPS. You navigated with an atlas, or you read the road signs. There weren't too many road signs on those back roads, but I really didn't care where I was going, as long as I was going somewhere. Finally, when I thought I had put enough distance between me and their party, I pulled off the road by a bridge and slept. The next morning, I was able to figure out where I was, so I headed for Pa. and home. I never saw either one of those kids again, nor did I care to. I suspect, when he reported to his ship, he may have been discharged after providing a positive urine sample for THC. I recalled the famous last words from my old CC just before we graduated. "If you want to succeed in your career, align yourself with those who are squared away. If you align yourselves with dirtbags, you will fail." I remember those words even now, thirty-seven years later, and I still live by them.

CHAPTER

13

Reporting for Duty

As soon as I got home, I went to dad's house and told him that I would be stationed at a small boat station just inside Ohio. He again seemed very interested and asked a lot of questions about where I would live and what my job would entail. I told him our primary mission is Search and Rescue, and our secondary mission is Law enforcement. He wanted to know about the boats, so I told him the one was a 41, foot UTB (utility tugboat), and the other was a twenty-two-foot Boston whaler. After I left his house, I stopped in at my brother's, and of course, answered many of the same questions. After that, I went to my sister Lydia and husband's house, where I would be staying during my ten days at home.

The following day, I went to the welding shop where I used to work. I knew most of the people there, so I was a little surprised when only a few of them said hello; the others just continued to do what they were doing with hardly a sideways glance. I couldn't help but get the feeling that things hadn't changed much since I left. Everyone seemed stuck in their old grind, and miserable. It was then, I remembered, this was why I left in the first place: miserable people stuck in a never ending, cultish cycle with no hope of ever leaving, so the only relief was back-stabbing and making fun of others, and now me, their main target, had just proven them all wrong. Instead of crawling back with my tail tucked between my legs, in failure, like a scolded dog, I had dared come back with my head held high, and a smile of success on my face. They knew by now that I was going to make it, and it must've grated every nerve in their bodies.

Day three of being around home, I began to get bored out of my mind, so I decided I would cut my leave short and report to my duty station. I simply couldn't take another day of this depressing area. So, I went to see Dad one more time and told him that I planned to leave early the next morning. He was a little sad, but still seemed to share some of my excitement, as I said goodbye and returned to my sister's place.

The next morning, I packed my few belongings, took a last look at the map, and struck out for Ohio, and my future. When you report to a new duty station, you are required to be in your dress uniform and have your orders in hand. If I had been reporting to a Cutter, I would have approached the ship, and before boarding, I would have saluted the flag, then the captain, then requested permission to come aboard. The small boat stations didn't require as much fanfare, mainly because the Officer in charge was normally an enlisted person, Chief Petty Officer, or higher, and we weren't required to salute an enlisted person.

My instructions were to park my car, then approach the station door. If no one came out to greet me, I was to knock on the door and wait until someone let me in. After that, I was to introduce myself rather smartly, something like this, "Seaman Apprentice Troyer, Reporting for Duty." That afternoon, when I was within a mile of the station, I pulled over along the road, I put on my tie and my dress jacket, checked to make sure my three ribbons were in a straight line, took a deep breath, and drove up a long winding lane into the parking lot.

As I got out, I was greeted by a third-class Petty officer named Bob and a Great Dane dog named Woody, the station mascot. Greetings were exchanged, Bob said that he was assigned as my mentor, and said he would introduce me to the others and show me around. He also said if I had any questions or concerns, I could always come to him. After that, he led the way inside.

It was a nice Station house, white with a red roof, typical Coast Guard colors. Inside was a recreation/meeting room of sorts, off to the side was an eating area with tables, behind the counter was a kitchen, across from the kitchen was the watch room, with a two-way Marine radio where the distress calls from the boats came in. Someone stood (sat) watch in this room twenty-four hours a day. On down the hall was the station commissary, where you could buy a few essentials if needed. Farther down the hall was the Chief and the XPO's (Executive Petty Officer) office. The XPO, was second in charge, below the Chief, then there was the OOD, (Officer of the day). This title switched to different higher-ranking Petty Officer's from day to day. The OOD was in charge of managing SAR calls. He also ran general operations on a daily basis, for instance, if anything out of the ordinary happened, or you needed to leave the base for any reason during duty hours, the OOD had to okay it. Another assigned position, which changed from one duty shift to another, was the duty Coxswain. This person was in complete charge of the boat when it went underway. Rank wasn't as important for this position. In other words, you could hold the rank of Seaman, as long as you were qualified. So, while underway, there was only one person that could overrule him, and that was the Chief, and before that would happen, the Coxswain would have had to commit an unforgivable dereliction of duty before the Chief would step in. To my knowledge, it had never happened at that station.

When I was introduced to the OOD, he signed my orders, which meant I was on duty from that moment. I didn't have to wait long to find out what I would be doing. Bob, my mentor, sat down with me and gave me a list of things I was expected to do while on duty. He informed me that because I was the newest Non-rate (Not a Petty officer), I was expected to clean the station house, including bathrooms and bedrooms, the floors had to be swept, mopped and buffed, at least once during each duty shift, and don't forget to empty the trash, and wash the dishes. I would also be going underway on the boat, as a boat crewman, in training. Every day, and on top of that, I would be sitting in the watch room for four hours each day, until qualified. Oh yeah, and anything else you're told to do. Bob may have been a little impressed when he saw that I was actually taking notes in a little note pad I carried in my pocket. After that, since it was getting late, he showed me where I would be sleeping. It was a bunk room with eight bunks. This was also where the boat crew slept while on duty. He told me to try to get some sleep because I would be sitting in the watch room from midnight until 0800. After that my day would start.

Our CC had told us, during the last week of Boot camp, what to expect. He told us that having a good attitude about all the menial tasks assigned to us would go a long way toward earning the respect of the senior crew members. He also reminded us that the crew would occasionally mess with us, like having us do stupid things, just to see if we would actually follow orders without question. He said just remember, they aren't picking on you, every one of them endured the same thing when they were new. I remembered those words, and it wasn't long, before I began to feel like I was one of them.

11:45, PM, I heard someone say my name. It took me a moment to figure out where I was, then it dawned on me, watch room! I rolled out of my bunk, brushed my teeth, then went down to the watch room. The person on watch told me to have a seat. I watched him go through his required check-off's before assuming his watch. He explained what he was doing as he did it. I couldn't help being fascinated by the whole thing. What I was learning seemed so, incredibly important. After all, people depended on us to save their lives.

Eventually, he asked the question I was expecting, "Is it true you were Amish?" I told him I was. Now it was his turn to ask questions, which he did for the next hour. At 5:45 AM, he announced on the intercom that it was time to for everyone to get up. The station began to come alive.

Soon the door opened and a Petty Officer dressed in white came in and said good morning. We were introduced. He said his name was Petty Officer Ramsey, and he was the Subsistence Specialist, in other words the cook. He began clanging around in the kitchen. The watchman told me to make a fresh pot of coffee for the crew, then help with breakfast if needed, so I did. Soon the XPO arrived, introduced himself, told me that after breakfast he would need to see me in his office to properly check me into the station and register me with the Group. The Group was the main Air Station in Detroit. All other stations, on Lake Erie, operated under their command, hence (The Group). By now the rest of the duty crew had their coffee in hand, and were sitting at the kitchen tables, chatting and bantering with one another. Finally, someone yelled, "Hey BOOT, we're out of Coffee." My CC had told me to expect to be called BOOT for as long as I was the newest member. He said just go with the flow, they're testing you. So, I smiled and hurriedly made a new pot of coffee. Last to arrive was the Chief. He looked a bit sullen as he walked in, muttered good morning to the crew, and entered his office. P.O. Ramsey and I finished cooking breakfast and laid it out on the counter cafeteria style. Ramsey then told someone to get the Chief.

The sailing services are steeped in deep traditions that started way back during the sailing vessel era, and many are practiced today. For one, you will not wear your cover (hat) inside, and especially not in the galley (Kitchen), reason being, during the early days, onboard ships, the wounded and dying were taken to the cleanest place on the ship, the galley, so out of respect to them, you are required to remove your cover when indoors, with one exception. If you are armed, you must wear your cover at all times.

Another tradition during the sailing ship era: the food mostly sucked. More times than not, the sailing crew was afraid to eat, because the rancid food could and would at times cause severe stomach illness, and even death. So, to help belay their fears, the captain would get his food first. When the crew saw that the captain didn't fall over dead, after eating it, they overcame their fear and ate it as well. That tradition is still practiced. The ranking Officer will go through the line first to get his food, then the Crew will follow. I was always interested in history, so these traditions and the reasons behind them captured my attention.

After breakfast, one of the other non-rates and I washed the dishes and cleaned up the Galley. The watchman yelled for me, so I went into the watch room. He told me that at 0800 every morning the Flag was to be raised while reveille was played on the loudspeaker. He told me to wait until reveille started playing, then briskly raise the flag to the top of the pole. After that, tie it off. If reveille wasn't finished playing yet, I was to stand at attention, and render a Salute to the flag until it stopped playing.

"Easy enough," he asked? I said, "Sure." I took the flag out and hooked it up. Shortly, reveille began to play, and I raised the flag. After tying it off, I rendered a Salute, then returned to the watch room. I was quite proud of my accomplishment. Now it was time for everyone to meet in the Rec. room for a morning meeting before starting work. We waited for some time for the Chief to show up. It seemed to take him a while to get there from his office. Finally, the door opened, and he came in and stood there for just a moment. I thought for some reason he didn't look exactly pleased. He said, "Who is the OOD?" One of the P.O.'s said, "I am, Chief." Then the Chief asked him, "Is this station under some type of duress, that I'm not aware of?" The OOD replied, "No Chief. Why do you ask?"

The Chief growled, "Because every EFFEN fisherman is calling me and asking if we're ok, APPARENTLY, our flag is flying upside down, somebody fix it, NOW." I froze for just a second, as everyone looked at me, I felt my face turning beet red, and I bolted out the door and out to the flag pole, lowering it, then raising it right side up. Of course, the fishermen in their boats took this opportunity to yell, "What a dumb ass." I ignored them as I ran back to the meeting. Everyone was laughing when I walked in. The XPO, took this opportunity to explain the meaning of an upside down flag (during the sailing vessel era, the ships didn't have radios, so if their vessel fell into distress, the captain would order the flag flown upside down. This was an international sign of distress to signal other vessels for help). He then reminded me of the importance of paying attention to detail. I assured him it would not happen again.

Every announcement over the station's intercom began with the word "NOW," apparently another tradition. Later that morning, I heard an announcement addressed to me, "NOW, Seaman apprentice Troyer, report to the XPO's office." I immediately stopped what I was doing and went to the XPO's office. He told me to sit down while he finished checking me into their system. During this time, he explained what I had to do to become watch room and boat crewman qualified. He gave me two rather large books and explained, "These are your study volumes, and in the back are your check-offs for your qualifications." I was to study the volumes and when I mastered some of the tasks, I was to ask the OOD of the day to quiz me, and if I could answer correctly, the OOD, would initial in the block. After some time had passed, and all my tasks were completed, then and only then, would I be able to sit in an oral board with several qualified P.O.'s whose job it was to grill me with questions. If I passed the oral board to their satisfaction, I would then be considered qualified either as a boat crewman or watchman. I was required to board for each position. Next, he told me that after one year I would be eligible for a promotion to the rank of Seaman, but first, I would have to order three volumes, study them, and pass a timed test. After that, when my year was up, I could be promoted. It seemed like a lot of studying, but I had an urge to get started, so I asked him to please order the volumes for me. He said, "That's a lot of studying, are you sure you can handle it?" I assured him I would be ready when the time came for testing, so he ordered them and dismissed me.

At 1000, if the workload permitted it, we were given a fifteen-minute break to grab a cup of coffee or a soda from the soda machine that we maintained for the station. The proceeds from the sodas were kept in a kitty for Veterinary bills and dog food for Woody, our mascot. When the XPO dismissed me, it was 1000, so I ran out to the garage where the soda machine was located. As I approached the machine, I noticed the Chief standing beside it, drinking a Pepsi. I nervously asked, "How are you, Chief?" I was still expecting some fallout from my recent flag incident, but to my surprise he simply asked where I was from. I told him I was from central Pa., he said he was from Milton Pa., and he then said that he noticed my last name, and that his dad used to take his farm implements to a Troyer's welding shop near Mt. Pleasant Mills. He wondered if I had ever heard of them. I told him that I had worked for them for five years. He replied, "Imagine that, so you were raised Amish?" I told him I was, then I said, "Nice talking to you, Chief, but I better get back to work." He said, "Ok, well, welcome to Fairport." I thanked him and fled back to my work area.

Station Fairport was a twenty-four-man station with two duty crews. The Chief, XPO, and the cook were day workers. They would show up in the morning and leave in the evening. The rest of the men were split into two duty crews. One crew would be on duty forty-eight hours. During that time they were required to eat and sleep at the station, then, after two days, the relief crew would arrive. All pertinent information would be passed to the incoming crew, then most of the outgoing crew would go home to their families for two days of liberty.

Since berthing was limited, only the two newest non-rates were allowed to live at the station permanently, then, when a new non-rate arrived, one or two of the permanent non-rates were required to get a two-bedroom efficiency apartment. And because the Government paid for the apartment, we were required to double up, to save money. So, for several weeks, another non-rate named Jon and I were the two permanent residence living at the station 24-7. We slept in the same berthing area as the duty boat crew, so even on our liberty days, we were subjected to constant intercom announcements, not to mention, the boat crew getting up all hours of the night, responding to (SAR) calls, (Search and Rescue). The most annoying thing I had to endure was the duty crew always commandeered the TV, and they were forever watching football, (I had no interest in football, I didn't grow up with it), so, to help minimize my annoyance, I would find a quiet place and immerse myself in my study volumes. I also spent hours in the watch room with the duty watchman, asking questions. I would ask him to please quiz me from the check-off list. Most of them didn't mind helping because it helped to break up their boring watch period. It wasn't long before I began to develop the reputation as a hard charger, eager and willing to learn, and as a result of my study habits, I began to get ahead of the other non-rates in my check off's. This didn't bode well with some of the other non-rates, but it did encourage some of them to step up their game.

I had been living at the station about two weeks and had most of my boat crewman and watchman volumes completed already when one day in walks a new non-rate, fresh from boot camp. His name was Steve Hamilton. He said he was from Bowling Green, Ohio. I introduced myself, then answered a few questions he had. In the coming days, we shared our duties and we seemed to work well together. Steve was an intelligent dude and seemed to be focused on getting ahead. I respected him for that, and over time we became friends, (it wasn't until days later, I learned that he was a brother to Scott Hamilton, the figure skating, Olympic Gold Medalist). He wasn't one to put on airs, but he did talk about his brother Scott to me. One day, he invited me to go to his home in Columbus, Oh. There, I met his father, a very kind man. We spoke for a while, then Steve showed me around the house, where he and Scott grew up. It was just a normal house, but nice and very comfortable.

Steve's arrival at the station put us over the quota of non-rates, so the XPO informed Jon and I that we were allowed to move into a two-bedroom apartment in a nearby town. I was ready to get away from the station and live in a quiet apartment, I just wasn't thrilled to be living with Jon. It's not like we were enemies, we just didn't always see eye to eye, and, since I didn't have a choice who my apartment mate would be, I decided to embrace the suck and try to make the best of it.

The first thing I needed was a bed. At that time, water beds were all the craze, and of course, the cheapest one was all I could afford. So, after buying one, I assembled it and filled it from an outside spicket with a garden hose. That night, when I crawled into my very own bed, it seemed to take forever to stop waving about. It reminded me of being underway in our boat. That was the first disappointment. The second disappointment came later that night, when I woke up shivering uncontrollably, I couldn't warm up, so I slept on the floor the rest of the night. The next day, the water had started to warm up to room temperature, and I was able to sleep the entire night with only moderate shivering. I also learned not to move much, to keep the wave action to a minimum. Two years later when I moved out, I bid adios to that bed and left it for the next unlucky inhabitant.

CHAPTER

14

Duty on the Lake

Afer several months of on the job training and getting all my checkoffs signed, I asked the OOD if I could have my oral board for watchman. He quizzed me one more time, then said he thought I was ready, so it was scheduled for the next day. The following day, three PO's and I sat in a circle, and they took turns firing questions and scenarios at me. After the board, which lasted almost an hour, the board leader told me that I did very well, then he signed the paperwork, stating that I was now qualified to be placed on the watch rotation. I felt very good. I had just passed another hurdle.

Several days later we again went through the same scenario, this time for boat crewman. I passed this as well. Now that I was fully qualified, I began to concentrate on my (Seaman) courses. I would study while sitting at the radio watch and while on my days off at the apartment. After a month or so, I told the XPO that I would like to take the test for Seaman. He asked me if I was sure, because I still had almost six months to go before I was eligible for promotion. I told him I thought I was ready, so he opened the safe and removed the test material, then gave it to me in his office. I finished the test in the allotted time, then handed it to him. After he finished grading it, he looked up at me and said, "You passed." Another hurdle passed, now all I had to do for a promotion was stay out of trouble and wait for the first year to pass by.

As time went on, and the summer boating season became busy, search and rescue calls increased as well. All of us became immersed in our jobs. I was having the time of my life in my new role as a member of the law enforcement boarding team. We would take the forty-one-footer on law enforcement patrols several hours of each day. We would pick a boat, any boat, then inform the captain to bring his vessel to a dead stop and prepare for a Coast Guard safety check. Once moored alongside of his vessel, the Petty Officer of the boarding team would go on board and check his flares, life jackets, and fire extinguisher. If everything checked out okay, we would issue a safety certificate, and send them on their way, all the while we were looking for drug paraphernalia, or drugs. If we saw any of those items laying in plain sight, we would then have probable cause to search the boat from top to bottom.

The Coast Guard had the authority to seize any vessel and arrest the people on board if any amount of drugs were found. The boarding team was armed with Colt 45's, 1911A1 Pistols. My job was to stand on the deck of our patrol boat and keep an eye over the whole operation. In addition to a pistol, I also manned a twelve-gauge riot shotgun loaded with double OO buck shot. My orders were that should everything head south and the team get overwhelmed by bad guys, I was to unleash the fury of the shotgun in an attempt to neutralize the threat. This I was prepared to do, should it become necessary. However, just the shear overwhelming fire power available seemed to quell any disturbances before they happened. I felt that I had found my niche. Law enforcement was what I enjoyed the most, so I looked forward to our boarding patrols.

Most of our rescues involved towing disabled boats back to the harbor. Others involved responding to boats taking on water. We had specialized pumps on our boat that we could utilize to pump water out of a sinking boat to keep it from sinking. If a boat sank before we could get on scene, then we rescued the people out of the water. In the unfortunate event someone drowned, the local authorities were notified to bring their dive teams on scene, but they were seldom successful, because of the lakes strong under currents.

We had it pegged, if someone drowned, and they didn't find the body, it would take exactly seven days for the body to float to the surface. We were than tasked with recovering the body for the coroner.

One morning while relieving the outgoing duty crew, they informed us that an older person was reported missing after telling his family that he was going to walk out the break wall to the light house. The on duty boat crew had searched for him but hadn't found him. The assumption was he had fallen into the lake and drowned. We quickly counted ahead seven days, and sure enough, it would fall on one of our duty days. Crap. No one enjoyed picking up dead bodies that were under water for seven days.

Right on cue, seven days later, the radio call we were dreading came through. "Coast Guard station Fairport, this is vessel so and so, channel sixteen, do you have a copy?"

"Motor vessel so and so, Station Fairport, switch to channel, two, two."

(Communications were established on the emergency channel sixteen, then switched to channel twenty-two in order to keep the emergency channel open.)

"Vessel so and so, Station Fairport, channel, two, two, send your traffic."

"Coast guard station Fairport, vessel so and so. We are one half mile east of the lighthouse, and there is a body floating out here, we will stand by and wait for you if you would like."

"Motor vessel so and so, Station Fairport, thank you for standing by, Coast Guard vessel 41432 is getting underway."

Hearing the SAR alarm sirens blaring was our cue to run to the boat and start the engines. As soon as the crew was on board, we threw the lines off and were underway. At this time, as was common, we still didn't know what or where the emergency was. Typically, we would find out once underway to save time. The Coxswain keyed the mike and announced, "Station Fairport, 41432, underway 4 POB" (people on board) "432, Fairport, we have a person in the water, one half mile east of the light house, vessel so and so is standing by on location."

"Fairport, 432, Copy."

We knew what that meant, the deceased had floated to the surface, so we began to prepare the Stokes litter for recovery. Unfortunately, the body wouldn't be able to get into the litter himself, so someone had to be volunteered to enter the water and roll the deceased into the litter.

The old saying is that crap rolls downhill. Well, it rolled down to me. Since I was the newest member on board, I got volunteered. I removed everything from my pockets, in preparation for a swim. When we arrived at the body, I lowered myself off the stern of our boat, and into the water. After swimming over to the body, the rest of the crew lowered the litter into the water, while I guided the body over to it, then dumped it into the litter as gently as I could. The crew then placed him on the deck and covered him with a blanket. After that, they helped me get back on board.

"Fairport, 432, person is recovered, enroute to Station."

"432, Fairport, coroner has been notified, he will meet you at the dock."

After tying up the boat, we turned the body over to the coroner. Then we scrubbed the boat with Clorox and soap to try to mitigate the smell. I can tell you with certainty, once you smell decaying human flesh, you will never be able to forget it, ever. That evening, after thinking over the day's events, I felt extremely fortunate to be where I was and to have the job I had. I was living a life of fulfillment. I would never have experienced any of this if I had decided to stay Amish.

Sometime during the first Summer, Jon said that he was going to get a tattoo. I told him I would like to get one too. So, we decided that we would go together after our duty shift. I knew how the Amish felt about tattoos, and maybe the reason I wanted one was to put even more distance between myself and the Amish.

The next day we went to a local tattoo parlor. The tattoo I picked was a wolf sitting under some pine trees, howling at the moon. This was the perfect tattoo for me since I had adopted the CB handle of the Lone Wolf. On the way home, I couldn't stop admiring my new ink. I was very proud of the fact that now I was really beginning to fit in. My Amish background was becoming more and more obscure with each passing day.

I must say, the first year flew by. We were so busy with SAR calls and law enforcement along with training requirements, I hardly noticed the time slipping by. Jon and I had both been promoted to E-3. I was now a Seaman.

After two years of service, we could attend our A-schools where we would learn our trades, and then, upon graduation, we would both be Petty Officer 3rd class a (noncommissioned officer). We did, however, have to finish one more year of service, without any disciplinary action taken against us. In other words, keep our noses clean.

I remember thinking, I won't have any problem keeping out of trouble for a year, after all I was focused on going to A-school, and nothing else really mattered. Then one evening after our duty shift was over, a bunch of us decided to go to a bar for dinner and a few drinks. I had no intentions of staying long. I had plans to get to my apartment early, to get my uniforms ready for the next shift, then relax a while and watch a movie.

It was while I was eating and sipping on an adult beverage that I noticed a dude at another table staring at me. I thought to myself, what a weirdo! I saw he didn't look any too friendly, I had never even seen him before, so, after a while I stopped looking at him, hoping he would find someone else to stare at. The next time I glanced his way, I noticed he was gone. Whew, what a relief.

Something hit me alongside of my head. I was already passing out as my chair went over backwards onto the hard dance floor, then, as my head hit the floor, I decided to finish passing out. After a few seconds, I started to regain consciousness and sit up. Then, out of nowhere came a cowboy boot to my chin. Well, time to pass out again. The next time I started to come to, I decided to assess my where-abouts before I raise my head. Then, through my blurry vision, I saw that same weird dude being held down by several off-duty cops.

Several of my buddies helped me up and took me outside, then one of them took me to the hospital. The doctor said, I must have a tough head, because he couldn't find anything wrong with me, so I was discharged and taken back to the Coast Guard Station for observation.

The next day I felt a little sore but okay otherwise. The Chief questioned me about the incident. I told him I had never seen the dude before in my life and had no idea what his problem was. He then told me to go to the police station and straighten everything out.

During the police interview, I found out this dude had a bone to pick with someone that he thought looked like me. It was a case of mistaken identity. I pressed charges, and he pled guilty to disorderly conduct.

I was sure this incident would prevent me from attending A-school, but the Coast Guard didn't hold me responsible and cleared me of all wrongdoing. After it was all over, there was really no harm done. Sure, my pride was hurt, and I was terribly aggravated that I never even had a chance to clobber the dude back. All I could do was pass out, over and over, it seemed. The guys at the station couldn't resist giving me a new nick name (Glass Jaw).

CHAPTER
15

Boatswains Mate School

The first year at Station Fairport was behind me. I thought about how fast it had gone by. It had been filled with training, work, and studies. Now that I was fully qualified, I found work to be extremely rewarding. In fact, I was having the time of my life, except for one thing: evenings and during my days off, I would become a little bored, so I asked PO Jeff Cooper, one of my go- to guys for advice, if there was anything I could do to enhance my training. He suggested that I enroll for a class at the local Community College. I was open to the idea, so I asked him what class he would recommend. He told me that if I take an EMT course, the Coast Guard would pay for it. So, off to the college I went. I signed up for evening classes and after eight weeks of that, and the required twenty hours of emergency room training, I received my EMT license for the state of Ohio. I was also registered with the Coast Guard as a qualified EMT. After that it was back to search and rescue and law enforcement as usual.

Training was always a part of our daily activities. It was important and helped keep us sharp and on our toes. I particularly enjoyed (Underway HELO. OPS.). Group Detroit would schedule the training day, then fly one of their helicopters to Fairport. We would then get underway with our forty-one-footer, and while underway at a moderate speed, the helicopter would hover overhead, matching our speed, then lower their litter down to the deck of our boat. After we pretended to put a person in it, they would pull it back up and into the helicopter. We performed this exercise several times until we did it well enough to impress the pilots, after which they would continue on to the next station. I simply couldn't get enough of seeing that beautiful orange and white helicopter, hovering thirty feet above our boat. I only wished the folks back home could see what I did for a living. The pride I felt serving in the Coast Guard never diminished. I still swell with pride when I think of my first enlistment and the thousands of things I was able to do for the first time. This was a lifelong dream, and I was living it.

At the time of my enlistment, I was required to pick what job I wanted to do. The recruiter presented me with a list of jobs that I was qualified for, then he explained what each individual job requirement was. For instance, damage controlman primarily worked below the deck, welding and repairing things; a Machinery Technician also worked below the deck, on engines; the Boatswains Mate, however, was a deck supervisor. This rating required you to know a little bit of everyone's job. A Chief Boatswains Mate, (Pronounced, BOSUNS Mate), was the captain's voice and was responsible for the overall appearance and operation of the vessel. He could also relieve the captain and man the bridge when the captain needed to sleep. It was also the only rating, at that time, that could be an Officer in charge of a Station, (OINC). It didn't take me long to decide where I wanted to be. I chose Bosuns mate.

Later, when I was promoted to Seaman, I applied for Bosuns Mate A-school. Then, early one morning in 1986, the Teletype (no E-mail yet) began typing an incoming message. The XPO handed the message to me and said, "Congratulations, Seaman Troyer, here are your orders to A-school." I was excited, but still a little apprehensive. This was another hurdle I had to overcome. I was to report to York Town Virginia the following June for ten weeks of intensive, non-commissioned Officers training. Upon graduation, I would be promoted to a Bosuns Mate 3rd class, or (BM3). But, before I could sign and accept the orders, I had to have twenty-four months left on my enlistment when I arrived at school. I was two months short, so the Chief came in to administer the oath. Once again, I raised my right hand and took the oath to serve my country an additional two months. I was now considered a short timer at this station, so all I had to do was basically kill time for the next month.

After I signed my orders, I decided to take a walk along the break wall out to the lighthouse one last time. As I walked I began to reflect over the last two years. I suddenly realized that my successes here at Fairport wasn't as much because of anything I did. I had to give the credit to the friends I made here. The Petty officers that took me under their wings and gently steered me down the right path. Many of the mistakes I made were often made not because of carelessness but because I simply didn't know. It seemed there was always a Petty Officer willing to extend a hand and help me get back on the path, such as PO Jeff Cooper, who taught me how to dress and how not to dress for different Holidays. PO. Putman, the old salt, who taught me a great deal about Seamanship and fanned the flames of adventure, encouraging me to go to far off places. PO, Bruce Richards and his wife, who invited me to their house for Christmas because they knew I didn't have anywhere else to go. PO, Ed Knepp, who taught me how to cuss like a sailor, and that it was okay to laugh. And above all, Chief PO. Don Moser (I didn't know this until much later) but, following our short visit at the soda machine, he informed both duty sections that if anyone screwed with Troyer, he would personally see to it that they suffered for it. As I returned to the station after my walk, I knew these people had become my family, and I would miss them dearly.

The week of my departure had finally arrived. Most of my belongings had already been packed in my car. Sometime, during the last year, I had traded my old Chrysler for a brand new Lynx Mercury with a standard shift. It was a bit smaller than my old car, so I had to pack it pretty tight. One of the PO's had scheduled a going away party for me at his house. Anyone was invited from the station that wanted to come. When I arrived, the PO, having it, asked for my car keys. As I handed them over to him, I ask him why he needed them. He said, "Tonight you're getting drunk, and you're not driving home." Now I've been buzzed before, but I was not one to intentionally get plastered. However in light of everything, that night I got a little plastered. NEVER again. It took me two days to recover from my hangover.

When the day arrived to leave, I said goodbye to the fellows, got in my car, and headed out the lane for the last time. I had taken a few days leave, so I could see my dad before heading on down to York Town Virginia. Ten weeks seemed like a long time to go to school, but the excitement was building. I was looking forward to being stationed at a new place after graduation. I had no idea where I was going, but my mind was set on Kodiak Island, Alaska. Support Center, Kodiak was the Coast Guard's largest base. It had its own Security Police Force, which is what I was aiming for, if at all possible.

Later that evening, I arrived at my sister's place, where I would be staying for a few days. After we ate dinner, I drove home to see Dad and my stepmother. By now I had been gone from the Amish for over two years. Everyone seemed to be getting used to the idea that I wasn't coming back. My own confidence was strengthened by the fact that I was making it on my own. There was no question about that. I was comfortable around the Amish, because I felt I had nothing more to prove, I wasn't just surviving, I was thriving. I had proven my point. There was nothing more to be said.

That evening, Dad seemed mildly excited for me. He asked a lot of questions about the school I was going to attend. I answered all the questions I could. I told him that I would be getting stationed somewhere else after graduation, but I wouldn't know where until afterwards. It was getting to be bedtime, so I told him I would come by to see him again before leaving for school, then I left. Over the next couple of days, I stopped in to see him as much as I could, but eventually the time came to leave for school, so I said goodbye with plans to leave for York Town the next morning.

I was on the road well before daylight, not because in was a long drive. It was only about a six-hour drive, but I wanted to arrive with plenty of time to check in, and, who knows, a flat tire could've made me late, and that is no way to arrive at a Military school. I arrived at the York Town base around midafternoon. I had to ask for directions to the school, where I was to check in. After checking in, a Petty Officer escorted me to a two-man room that I would share with another student for the next ten weeks. He then handed me a piece of paper with directions to the school, the chow hall, etc. along with rules to be followed while staying at their facility.

He told me that we, the students, were expected to stand four-hour watches at the front door, and also down by the training boats, but only during the night. He said that we would be taking turns as watch Captains. I was familiar with the militaries policies of having a live watchman during low visibility hours, so this was no surprise. We were no longer recruits, therefore, we were no longer treated as such. All of the students had a minimum of two years of service, some had more, so we were treated as fellow sailors, who were supposed to be Petty Officer material. After all, that was the reason we were there.

That evening my roommate wandered in, and after stowing his gear, we decided to go to the chow hall for dinner where we exchanged stories of our last duty station. He was also from a small boat station, so we had a lot in common and had many of the same experiences. The following morning, we met in the classroom. There were close to a dozen students. I don't recall exactly how many, but enough to make it interesting. The instructors introduced themselves first. After that we took turns standing and introducing ourselves and telling them whether we were from a small boat station, or from a ship. I would say we were split about even. The instructors said that the small boat guys would have a lot of knowledge about the forty-one-foot UTB's, and that we should be ready to share our knowledge with the Shipboard guys to help them out, and vice versa. Fortunately for us, the school had a fleet of forty-one-footers that we would be training on.

We were told that the first couple of weeks would be mostly classroom training, and during that time we were required to pass the dreaded Rules of the Road with a 90%, or higher. These rules had nothing to do with the road, that was just what they were called. They had everything to do with navigating the high seas and inland waters. We had to learn all the dozens of buoys, their colors, and what they meant, what boats and ships had the right-of-way;

it covered all International waters as well. Let's just say, there was a boat load of knowledge to absorb. Besides the navigational rules, we would take turns plotting courses on a chart through the Chesapeake Bay, then give directions to the student driving, while below deck, looking only at the radar. We had man overboard drills, cold water survival training, leadership training, etc. We practiced everything, over and over, until it became second nature.

The 10th and final week was test week. We were tested on everything that we practiced during the nine weeks prior. We were allowed one fail. After that, you had better pass, or you wouldn't graduate and would have to apply for another ten weeks of school.

To me the school was fun, but not fun enough to do it for the second time. Also, during the last week, we were allowed to submit a dream sheet, listing places where we would like to go. Most students listed six places on their dream sheets. The instructors would go down the list, and the first one that had an opening is where they would send you. I wrote Kodiak Alaska in all six slots of my dream sheet, and of course the instructors had to mess with me. They tried to keep a straight face when they told me there were no openings on Kodiak. I knew by their grins that they were lying, and I told them so. After they couldn't hide it anymore, they finally told me, "Seaman Troyer, you're going to Kodiak Alaska, Base Security." I was elated. That was exactly what I had hoped for.

At the end of the tenth week, we were given our orders to our new stations. Some had orders to a ship, others to small boat Stations. I had orders to Kodiak Alaska. After a short graduation ceremony, the instructors came down the line and pinned our Chevron insignia to our collars. They then called us up one at a time to present us with our diplomas. When I heard them call Petty Officer Troyer, I approached the podium, shook hands, and received my diploma. After the ceremony, we were dismissed, and free to go.

That afternoon I packed all my belongings in my car, said goodbye to my school mates, and headed for home. I had taken several days of leave with the intentions of driving to New York to visit my sister and some of my cousins, not knowing when I would ever see them again, since I was going way up to Alaska. That evening I arrived at my sister's place, and after staying the night,

I drove up to see my dad and stepmother. Dad seemed excited to see me as usual, even though he had to shun me because of the Amish. I knew that he was concerned about my wellbeing, and that I was deeply missed.

Dad and I wrote letters back and forth constantly. It was only after his death that I learned that he had carefully packed away every letter I had ever written to him. When I told him where I was being stationed, he appeared a little sad, but still excited, so much so, in fact, that he immediately got his road Atlas out, so he could pinpoint where I was going. He also told me to make sure I write him often and tell him what Alaska was like. I promised him that I would.

After a while, he wanted to know how I was going to get there. I said that the plan is to drive to Seattle, Washington, put my car on a Ferry boat to Kodiak, then fly to Anchorage, and from there to Kodiak Island. It would take a week or more for my car to arrive. After a lengthy visit, I told him goodnight and that I would see him before I headed west. For me it was always very hard to say goodbye to Dad. He was getting older, and it always crossed my mind that I might never see him again, and, although I had chosen a different path in life, I still loved my father very much, and I was keenly aware how deep his love was for his youngest son, and for that reason, saying good bye would always be painful for both of us.

The next day I drove the eight hours north to Norfolk, N.Y., where my Cousins lived, and where I lived for two years. My sister Lovina and her husband still lived there. I had plans to visit them and also some of my old friends. I had no idea how I would be received by them, so I was prepared for the worst. I was surprised when most of them seemed happy to see me. After all, it had been over two years since I had left the Amish. I was aware that they were required to shun me—that would never go away, so I tried to not put them in a position where they would be uncomfortable. I stayed in a motel, and when it got close to mealtime, I would make an excuse to go to town for a while. Overall, my visit to N.Y., I felt, could not have gone better, and I was glad that I went.

When I returned to Pa. I went to see Dad for the last time before heading to Seattle. I wanted to give myself plenty of time to get there, because I wasn't sure how long the trip would take. Up until that time, I had only been as far west as Missouri. That was the first time I left the Amish. I was only eighteen years old at the time. So, this time, I was really looking forward to my journey. I had read about many places throughout the west, in western books, and I was excited to finally see some of them.

Following a tearful goodbye with my dad and brothers, I finished packing my car with all my guns and other less important stuff and headed west toward Seattle. The drive started out semi-boring. Ohio and Indiana were both rather Ho-Hum, then I hit Chicago. I hated that city. It reminded me of driving through N.Y. city, I'll just tell you, it sucked! After I finally got through it, into Wisconsin, the countryside began to open up, and I started enjoying the drive. As a child I had read the Huckleberry Finn and Tom Sawyer books, so crossing the Mississippi river into Minnesota had special meaning to me. Not to mention, after crossing the Mississippi, I felt I was finally in the west. Minnesota didn't really look like what I had imagined the west would look like, but it was still interesting to see the bluffs. Finally as I drove through western Minnesota and crossed into South Dakota, I couldn't stop smiling. Finally the great plains, names of Indian Tribes that I recognized from reading western books, cities like Sioux Falls, Rapid City, all of them began to feed my imagination.

South Dakota, I found, was an extremely long state, and I began to wonder if I had given myself enough time to make it to Seattle, so I didn't stop to sight see as much as I would have liked. Rolling across the Wyoming State line was a little euphoric. City names like Sundance and Cheyenne were so familiar to me, however, I had of course only read about them.

I decided to try to make it to Sundance for the night. I remembered reading about the Sundance Kid and thought it would be cool to stay there. Later that evening I arrived in Sundance. After checking into a motel, I walked across the street to a bar for something to eat and a beer. While eating my dinner, I struck up a conversation with several locals who told me that there was a small museum down the street that had some old western memorabilia on display from The Sundance Kid and General Custer. The next morning, before taking off, I went to the museum, and sure enough, there was a leather shirt on display, claiming to have been owned by General Custer. Also some old Sheriffs badges and a few items owned by The Sundance Kid. At least that is what it said. I don't know if it was all true or not, but I liked the idea.

I must say, when I finally crossed into Montana, I was convinced that this was the most fun I had in my lifetime, and to think if I hadn't left the Amish, I probably would never have seen the west, and now I was driving right through the Crow Indian reservation. Later I crossed the Little Bighorn River, the, Yellowstone River, and then the Continental Divide. It was like a whole new world to me, and then I saw a sign pointing to Custer's Last Stand. I simply couldn't resist stopping, so I followed the sign to a small museum. Inside was a table of sorts with a miniature landscape on it, explaining how Custer's Last Stand unfolded, in great detail. I found this extremely fascinating. Later, while driving through western Montana and into Idaho, I knew that it was the most beautiful scenery I had ever seen. I made a mental note to myself that this would be an awesome place to live someday.

The following day, I drove through Washington state. I wasn't too thrilled by the scenery, just wheat field after wheatfield, it seemed, until I got close to Seattle, then I began to see some mountains again. When I was about forty miles from my destination, I noticed that my car was losing power. It started sputtering and wheezing. The engine was missing and carrying on something awful. I didn't know much about cars at that time, so I pulled into a garage and they began checking it out. After a while they said it was fixed. It needed a new spark plug wire. Sure enough, it ran fine when I hit the road. Later that afternoon I dropped my car off at the Ferry Terminal and hired a taxi to take me to a motel. I was scheduled to fly to Anchorage, Alaska the next morning. In those days, GPS was unheard of, so all my navigation was done with half-assed directions and a road atlas. I still don't know how I found where I was going, but somehow, I did it.

The next morning, after checking my luggage, I boarded the plane for Alaska. It still amazes me when I think back at how relaxed everyone was. People were laughing and having a good time, smoking was still allowed on planes, there were minimal restrictions, and people could actually enjoy themselves while traveling. I for one loved to fly, though not anymore; now I hate it.

The flight to Anchorage seemed to take forever but was only around four hours. I was anxious to get there. I could hardly wait to see Alaska. Just the fact that it was called the last frontier intrigued me. Eventually the pilot made an announcement that we were flying over the Canadian Rockies. When I looked out the window, I was totally awestruck at the snow-covered mountains below us, which were breathtakingly beautiful. Eventually the plane landed in Anchorage. It was a clear sunny June day. After I got off the plane, I went over to Era Aviation, where I was scheduled to board a flight to Kodiak Island. When I walked up to the counter, I was told that all flights to Kodiak were canceled because of weather. I mentioned that the weather looked fine to me. She laughed, and said, "This must be your first time to Kodiak." I told her it was. She smiled and said, "You'll get used to the weather." She also said, that when the cloud cover falls to 2,000', the Kodiak Airport closes. She told me that a flight would be leaving in the morning, and she would schedule me for that one. I thanked her, then found a payphone and called the base to tell them that I wouldn't be there until the next day. I was sure they would be upset, but they didn't seem to be. They just said, "Get a motel. We'll see you tomorrow if the weather breaks."

It was early afternoon, so I hailed a taxi to take me to a motel so I could lock up my belongings. I intended to do a little sightseeing while I had the chance, so, after getting a shower and change of clothes, I decided to go for a walk and get something to eat. The fact that I was in Alaska seemed almost surreal, like I was living in a dream. Oh wait, I was living a dream.

After finding a restaurant that appealed to me, I sat down and ordered dinner. When the waitress brought my food out, I couldn't believe how much food was on my plate. There was no way I was going to eat all that, so I ate what I could, then, after walking back to my room, I decided to turn in a little early.

The following morning, I hitched a ride on the motel taxi back to the airport. This time the flight didn't get canceled, and soon we were airborne.

It wasn't a long flight. When we touched down on Kodiak, what a thrill. I wouldn't be leaving this place for two years.

I was met at the airport by P.O. John French. He was to be my mentor. His job was to help me get checked into the base. I loaded my belongings in his Security Patrol Vehicle, and we headed to the base. As we approached the main gate, a Security Patrolman motioned us through. Soon we arrived at the Base Security headquarters building, where I would get my orders signed.

When we walked in, the first thing I saw was the dispatcher's desk. There was a two-way radio, a couple of computers, and a telephone. Behind the desk sat a Security Patrolman. As I approached the desk with my orders, he looked up at me and in a deep Southern accent, he said, "Hi, I'm Lennard Roberson, (Pronounced Lennart, in the south), if you like to hunt and fish, you'll like it here."

I introduced myself and assured him that I enjoyed hunting and fishing. He then asked, "Where ya'll from? I'm from Gorgia." I told him I was from Pa. After that he said, "After you get settled in a couple of days, we'll get together and fish. The Pink Salmon are starting to run."

That conversation started a friendship that's lasted for thirty-five years now. Next John took me to the base housing, where I was assigned a room. He told me to get settled in, then call base Security, and someone would pick me up for lunch. After that, I would be issued my Security uniforms. He also said that since my car wasn't going to be here for another two weeks, I would be picked up for work in the mornings and taken back to my room at night. It was then I began to see the benefits of being a Petty Officer, and I was liking it.

That afternoon I was issued my uniforms and introduced to what the job duties would be. As a security Patrolman, we would man the main gate 24-7, in four-hour shifts. We would run radar for speeders, break up fights at the bar, respond to domestic violence calls, and apprehend drunk drivers. Our jurisdiction was anywhere, on Government property, to include the main road from Kodiak City, where it crossed Base property. I was required to work with a trained person, as I trained on the job. Our duty shift was as follows, 4 days on, 4 days off, then 4 nights on, 4 days off, it was without a doubt, the best duty schedule, I would ever experience in all my life, in short, our duties were the same as any other Peace Officer. I could hardly wait for morning, when I would start my training, Law enforcement was my thing.

Early the following morning, I called for a ride. After a few minutes, my ride arrived and took me to the Administration Building, where we were based out of. The watch Captain told us to go eat breakfast at the Chow hall, then I was to go to the gate for a shift of four hours. Of course I would be training only, with a regular guard. After finishing my four-hour shift, I would ride with various Patrolmen, as they showed me the area. It was mostly on the job training, and it would last several months. And again there were volumes to study, with check off's, followed by an oral board.

CHAPTER

16

Life on the Rock

After a few months of training, I was getting quite good at my job. I found this type of work very appealing, so I seemed to pick it up quite fast. I was almost ready for my oral board. After two weeks of catching rides back and forth, I received a phone call from the ferry dock in Kodiak that my car had arrived, so I hitched a ride to town, signed some papers, then drove my car to the base. Now that I had my own wheels, I couldn't wait to explore the only road on Kodiak, the only road that went anywhere, that is. Up until now, on my days off, I had to rely on my friend Lennart to take me fishing, which he did. He was also generous enough to take me to his house in Kodiak, where he and his wife Heidi lived. Their southern hospitality was abundant. They insisted that I eat with them often. That is where I was first introduced to Southern sweet tea. Wow, did I love that stuff. There was a pitcher of tea in their fridge that never seemed to get empty. Lennart and I spent a great deal of time together. He always had some type of boat. It wasn't always very seaworthy, but it did get us out on the water. We weren't always sure that we would make it back to shore, but somehow, we always did. The first year I was in Kodiak, deer season rolled around, and I hadn't been in Alaska long enough to buy resident hunting license, but I was able to buy Nonresident Antlerless deer license over the counter for a reasonable price. Lennart said that he heard there were deer on an Island about a mile off shore called Spruce Island, so he asked if I would be interested in going over there for a day and see if we could find some.

He said we would take his boat over as long as the seas were calm. Now mind you, Lennart's boat wasn't very big, and the motor was even smaller, and on top of that, his boat liked to leak a little water in around the seams, especially when you weren't paying attention. I told him I was in, as long as the seas were calm, so, it was a go. The next morning we launched into the big old ocean and headed for Spruce Island. The seas were flat calm, but the day was overcast. After a half hour of skimming along at about three miles per hour, it was time to bail some water, I had gotten pretty good at bailing while under way, so I grabbed the cut off jug, meant for bailing to begin dipping water. Now, when Lennart saw me grab the bailing jug, he would automatically lean to one side, so as not to get a face full of flying water, it was all routine, no big deal, we had developed a working system. After about an hour of bailing, and skimming along, we finally reached the shore at Spruce Isl.

We saw very little sign of any deer the first half of the day, and we were starting to get discouraged, so we decided to sit for a spell and eat our lunch. It was during this time that we saw a doe poke her head over a knoll about eighty yards away and commence staring at us.

Lennart looked at me and asked, "Do you think you can hit her?" I said there was only one way to find out, so I laid my sandwich down and took a rest on my knee. After settling the crosshairs on her forehead, I lit one off in her direction. Lennart said he didn't know if I got her or not, she just vanished.

I finished eating my sandwich, then we hiked down where we had seen her head poking up. There she lay, with a bullet hole square between her eyes. I was pretty happy to have filled my tag. We were both reliving the hunt as we dragged her down toward the shore where the boat was. As we neared the shore it began to rain. We also noticed the wind had picked up a little. By the time we finally reached our boat, she was bucking up against the shore with every wave that came in. Also the wind and rain had reached gale force by now.

We had two choices. We could stay there for the night with no fire or food and hope it would let up enough the next day for us to return to Kodiak, or we could throw caution to the wind and make a run for it. Being seafaring men like we were, we decided we would rather die at sea than die from Hypothermia, huddled under some pine tree, on Spruce Isl.

We had unanimously decided that dying at sea would be the preferred method, so we unceremoniously dumped the deer into the boat. I baled in on top of her, while Lennart positioned himself in the Captain's seat and sputtered the little motor to life. I grabbed the bailing jug as Lennart throttled up that little motor to its screaming max and headed for the high seas at a breakneck speed of about one mile per hour.

I heard Lennart screaming about getting more weight to the front of the boat, and that the motor didn't have enough ass to get us up on plane. I grabbed the deer and hung her out over the front of the boat, than I laid on top of her, backwards, with my feet hanging over the bow. This way I could still bail water between the waves coming over the side and the driving rain.

It was necessary to keep bailing as fast as I could. When we finally reached the halfway point, we were hitting four foot waves. We were taking on water with every wave. I trusted Lennart's boating skills, but when I saw the concerned look on his face, I thought maybe this was an overreach. I decided to keep bailing as long as I we had some freeboard showing. I also liked the fact that I was riding backwards. It meant I couldn't see the end coming. After what seemed like an excruciatingly long time of hovering somewhere between life and death, I noticed the lines of concern on Lennart's face beginning to soften. Shortly thereafter I felt the boat bump against the dock. Lennart left out a big sigh and said, "You can stop bailing now, we made it." That, unfortunately, wouldn't be my only near death experience with my dear friend Lennart.

Over time I made even more friends. Tim Mauldin, from North Carolina, Bob White, from North Carolina, then there was Dale Weigand from somewhere in Wisconsin. Now for some reason Lennart didn't really get along with those three, and they didn't exactly see eye to eye, with Lemert. I got along well with all of them, which put me in a rather good spot. Whichever group had the best plans for our four-day liberty, that's the group I would tag along with. There were so many outdoorsy things to do on Kodiak. If the weather was going to be decent, the three amigos and I would take the boats over to near Island, about a mile from Kodiak, where we would camp for several days at a time. It was an interesting Island. There were a lot of Quonset huts, and some falling down buildings, abandoned after WWII. No one lived on the island, so we had the run of the place. We would hunt Snow Shoe Hares with our pistols or bow and arrows. There was a small lake where we would fish for Trout. It was just an awesome time.

Another place we would often go was a place called Sultry Cove. We could drive there, but just barely. It was fourteen miles of the most rugged trail/road that you could imagine. Some places the road leaned so hard, we would all hang off the uphill side of the trucks to keep them from tipping over. Then there were the mud holes to go through, most of them, you could just gun it and slog on through, but there was this one particularly deep hole where the roof of some hapless vehicle was sticking out of the mud about midway through, this mud hole was a bit tricky to cross, to be successful, you had to get enough speed to make it to the sunken vehicle, then bounce off its roof, this would give you enough momentum to hit the other side.

Kodiak was no place to have a new truck. Beater trucks were always in high demand. Tim Mauldin had one such beater. In fact when he bought it, it had already been rolled and had crinkles all over it, along with a leaky gas tank, so, Tim and I went searching through some wrecked and abandoned boats for something that we could make a gas tank out of. We eventually found an old metal hydraulic tank that we saw as holding potential, so, after cleaning it up, I welded some fittings to it, then we mounted it in his pick-up bed, and that became his gas tank. Now you are probably wondering why we didn't just buy a new tank. Well here is why: everything had to be shipped to

Kodiak, mostly by plane, so if you would order parts, you would expect to pay twice as much because of shipping. That is why, on Kodiak, old trucks seldom died, and if they did, they were soon parted out.

Kodiak was one of those places that you either loved or you hated. I loved everything about it. I loved the fact that it was not easy to get to, which discouraged a lot of people from wanting to live there. Sure it had its down sides too. In the summer it was overcast and rained a lot. In the winter, the days were very short and overcast a lot of the time. It didn't get terribly cold though, but we did get a fair amount of snow. We learned that to enjoy The Rock, as it was called, you couldn't let the weather discourage you. If it was raining you wore a rain suit and pursued your activity of choice. In the winter, you hunted deer, or trapped fox, and if the weather got too crappy, the base had a wood hobby shop and an auto hobby shop, free to use. They had all the tools for you to sign out and work on your vehicle. It was a great setup for the base.

One day, Tim Mauldin started belly aching that he didn't have a trailer to haul his Zodiac inflatable boat, and getting it on the back of his pick-up was a real pain in the ass. I told Tim that we should just build a trailer for him. He didn't really know where to start, so I told him to go to the junk yard and find a rear axle and springs from a pick-up. Then he, Dale, and I would meet at the auto hobby shop, where they had a welder, cutting torch, and grinder.

After Tim found a suitable rear end with springs, he called me, and we agreed to meet Saturday morning. I had a lot of experience fabricating metal from when I worked at Troyer's welding shop, so I was looking forward to this build. After we met at the shop, I began to take measurements. Tim and Dale did the cutting to length while I welded. After several hours, we had us a flat-bed trailer frame. We still needed a floor, so we towed it to the wood hobby shop and bolted a wooden deck on it. In less than a day we had constructed a very decent looking and usable trailer. Tim used that trailer until he left the island several years later. I have no doubt that trailer is still somewhere on that island. Someone may even be using it yet.

After living in the barracks on base for about a month, the barracks manager approached me and asked if I would be willing to find an apartment in town. He was running low in rooms for some new non-rates that were scheduled to arrive, and, since the government paid for the apartment anyway, I told him that I would try to find one. It had to be an efficiency apartment and had to meet the allotted price the government would pay.

Someone told me to check at Spruce Cape Apartments, in downtown Kodiak. They had one available, so I rented a single bedroom with a small kitchen and living room. It wasn't very nice by any standards, but it suited me just fine. It gave me even more freedom to come and go than living on the base. It wasn't long until I became friends with the manager of the complex. When I told him that I used to build houses with my dad, he asked if I would consider being his Assistant Manager. He offered to pay me quite well, so I told him I would help him out on my days off if I wasn't doing fun stuff. He said that that would work, so we had a deal. My job was to clean, make repairs, and paint every time someone moved out of an apartment. I was to do this as soon as possible, so he could move someone else in. It was sort of a fun job, especially during the long dark winter months. It helped to pass the time and put a fair amount of extra money in my pocket. I did that until I left Kodiak two years later.

After about four months of on the job training, I had not only been exposed to nearly every scenario, short of using deadly force, I had been handling most of the situations we encountered, under the watchful eye of my ride along, I had taken such an interest in Law Enforcement that I felt confident in my abilities to handle most incidents. It must have shown, because my ride along informed the watch Captain that I was ready for my board, so the following day I sat down with the three Special Investigators, and they took turns grilling me with every conceivable scenario, and I had to explain what action or re-action I would take. Finally, after an hour of questions, they told me I was fully qualified and pinned badge number 117 on my chest. About a month later, I was assigned as the new ride along Training officer for all new arrivals to our shift. I didn't mind the extra responsibilities. I soon realized that training others kept me at the top of my game, and that is where I wanted to be.

Name   S.S. TROYER
Title SECURITY PATROLMAN
Badge No.   117

Signature of Bearer

J.S. BLACKETT
Commanding Officer
U. S. Coast Guard Support Center
Kodiak, Alaska

No.   117

Security Patrolman, Badge ID. 1987

It was a dreary day with low overhanging clouds. Barometer Mountain, about a mile inland from the airport, was covered in clouds. Only the base of it was visible. I was on routine patrol along Base Town Road when my two-way radio keyed up and the Watch Captain announced, "Base, All Units, Return to base."

I replied, "Base, 117, Copy."

I knew something significant must have happened that couldn't be announced over the radio. Sure enough, after we had all returned to base, the watch Commander informed us that Kodiak Airport had reported that a fighter jet from the Anchorage Air force Base was doing touch and go landings at the Kodiak Airport, and that after his last takeoff, they lost all radio contact with him, and they suspected he may have crashed somewhere in the vicinity of Barometer Mountain. Anchorage confirmed that the plane had not returned and cautioned that the plane was fully armed with munitions, and should we find a crash site, all steps must be taken to keep the public away from it.

We were instructed to patrol all roads around Barometer Mountain while the Special Investigators gathered a search party and searched the entire mountain. Normally, the Coast Guard would have launched a helicopter to do the search, but couldn't this time because of the low-hanging clouds, so the search had to be done on foot. We continued patrolling the bottom of the mountain while the search party hiked up the face through the dense fog. Eventually, after several hours, the search captain confirmed our fears when he reported that the package had been found, and there were no survivors. They collected as much of the pilot as they could find, placed him in a body bag, and carried him down the mountain. For the next several weeks we had to routinely patrol the area to keep nosey people from climbing up to the crash site, while the military did their crash investigation. Apparently, the pilot saw the mountain a little too late. He tried to turn, but was traveling too fast to clear, and crashed belly first into the mountain. After several months, the wreckage was cleared, and we were able to return to normal patrols.

When I first arrived on Kodiak, I changed my residency to Alaska but wasn't considered a resident able to buy a hunting license until I lived there for a year, June of 1988 was my first-year anniversary, so I entered a drawing for a Mountain Goat tag. I knew guys that had applied for years, and never been drawn, so I was surprised when I was notified that I had been successful and had drawn a tag. I began to plan a hunt for that fall. Meanwhile Lennart and I fished our hearts out during the Salmon runs. We also set a string of crab traps in Old Woman's Bay that we would check almost every day.

I love sea food, and that summer was filled with seafood. All the Crab and Smoked Salmon I could eat. Life was so good. Later that fall, Tim, Dale and I, along with a few other guys, chartered two bush planes to take us to the other side of the Island for a two-week deer hunt. I was literally having the time of my life.

Later that fall, after getting almost two feet of snow, Lemert asked if I wanted to go Ptarmigan hunting with him and a friend named Mike. It was a beautiful, sunny day, so I said I would love to. We drove about twenty miles along a dirt road until we found a mountain we thought should have some Ptarmigan on it. We had some snacks along, but since it was only a day hunt, we left them in the truck. After slogging through two feet of snow up the mountain, we found that the snow was much deeper on top. We discovered that the only way to not sink to our waists was to step on the limbs of Alder bushes, which acted as snow shoes, and in this fashion we continued to hunt, out over the mountain and down the other side, into a saddle, where we decided to rest a bit, and since our clothes were wet anyway, we just sat in the snow to catch our breath.

After sitting there for a few minutes, in true Kodiak fashion, the sun simply disappeared. A few minutes later, it began to rain, and a bank of pea soup fog engulfed the entire mountain. Now, we weren't rookies to Kodiak weather, but that day we were woefully unprepared. GPS was still a thing of the future. In those days, we hiked by our instincts, or with a compass, provided we didn't forget our compass like we did that day. The fog was so dense, we could hardly see each other, let alone any landmarks, so we started walking in the direction that seemed the most right. After several hours of slogging through waist-deep snow, and soaked to the bone, we were exhausted, we didn't have food or water, and our situation was fast becoming life threatening. We had turned toward the direction we thought the ocean was in, knowing that the road followed the ocean. To maintain this direction, we had to hike around the side of the mountain, so our next concern was we could easily fall into one of the many deep ravines washed into the side of the mountain.

The light was fading fast, we were soaking wet, and completely exhausted. It was obvious we would be spending the night in the brown-bear infested Kodiak wilderness, in the rain and wet snow. We had enough cold weather training to know the likelihood of surviving a fourteen-hour long night in our condition, without a fire, was slim.

It was time to make a plan, so we took inventory of what we had on us. Lemert had a canvas wallet with a few dry dollar bills, Mike had a few emergency flares and a flare pistol, I had a pack of semi dry book matches, a space blanket, and a small candy bar. We decided that we would have the best chance of surviving if we headed straight down the mountain and attempted to start a fire, so down the mountain we went. Lennart and Mike were both married, and their wives had a general idea where we were going to hunt. At least they knew what road we were on. Our hope was when we didn't return, they would call the Coast Guard, and maybe they would launch a helicopter to search for us. Later, they told us that they did call the Coast Guard, but were told they couldn't fly because of the dense fog.

It was dark when we finally reached the bottom of the mountain where we found a pine tree, which gave us a little protection from the incessant rain. There was a small stream where we finally got a drink.

We knew the dangers of contracting Beaver Fever from drinking the water but figured we could survive that better than death. Also along the stream was a very distinct bear trail, which didn't help put us at ease. At this point, it was survival of the fittest, and we still had our shotguns. This we hoped would make us the fittest, should an altercation arise between us and a bear.

The first thing we needed to do was get a fire going, if possible, so I took my emergency space blanket out of its pack for the first time. I was disappointed how small it was. It was only about 30" by 30" and made from the same material as a party balloon. We than made a frame by poking sticks in the ground, then we stretched the flimsy space blanket over them to form a makeshift roof in the hopes of keeping the rain from dousing our fire. The only firewood available was green alder limbs that we could break off with our hands. We didn't have a light, so we had to feel our way around in the dark. When we had a sufficient amount of green twigs, Lennart fished out his dollar bills and tried to light them. They didn't burn very well, so next he tried to light his canvas wallet with the remaining matches. We were down to the last match when the wallet slowly began to burn. Lennart then lay down beside the small flame a blew on it for a very long time, finally some of the wet twigs began to burn. We were never able to get more than a moderate flame because of the wet wood and rain. Oh yes, the space blanket, the first small wave of heat, crinkled that thing into a worthless little ball. I remember thinking the person that invented that worthless piece of crap should be shot and likely would have been had he been there that night.

We took turns lying beside the fire, one hour at a time, while one of us would be breaking branches, the other stood bear watch with a shotgun. In this fashion, we were able to survive a long and grueling, shivering night, in the Kodiak wilderness. The next morning, as soon as it became daylight enough so we could walk without falling, we cut my little candy bar into three equal pieces and ate it. We decided to follow the stream, knowing that it would empty into the ocean. We also knew the road followed the ocean, so sooner or later we would find our way out. After hiking for several hours, we saw a tiny speck in the distance that looked like a human, so one of us fired a shotgun into the air to get their attention. It worked, the speck waved at us, and we knew we were found. When we got to the road, an Alaska State Trooper gave us a ride up to our truck, where a search party had formed. They had just started following our tracks when the Trooper called them back. After everyone knew we were alive, the Trooper gave us a ride back to base. Lemert, wasn't feeling well so he went to the base Hospital, where he was treated for excessive smoke inhalation. Apparently, he had inhaled some smoke while blowing on the fire. The following day, I drove Lennart out to retrieve his truck. On the way I thanked him for being so persistent with the fire. It may have been the only thing between us and death from hypothermia. Fortunately, we will never know, but many people have died from far less exposure to the elements than what we endured that night. Lennart and I agreed that we had been way under prepared, so we decided to each put together a survival pack and never go for even a short hike without taking it along, so that's what we did, and of course, we never needed it.

Getting Stationed on Kodiak was by far the best decision I could have made. I had never experienced anything quite like this place, the hunting and fishing were by all accounts, amazing, I enjoyed my job, the duty shift was awesome, I was simply in love with the place, and I could easily have spent the rest of my life there. Sure, it had a few downsides, such as it rained a lot, and every month or so there would be an earthquake. Generally not huge, but you could feel them, and every now and again, one would actually rattle the dishes in my cupboard. earthquakes were by all standards a pain in the ass for the Security Patrolmen. Every time one would hit, every one of us would be recalled to the base, day or night, on or off duty. We had to report to the base, and our focus was to evacuate the entire base, just in case a tsunami may have been generated. We had forty-five minutes to evacuate the base. The helicopters would go airborne, and the ships would head out to sea until the danger was over, then everyone would return to normal.

Early one morning, while sleeping at my apartment, I woke up to a rocking motion at the same time the dishes in my cupboard began to rattle, slowly at first, then faster and faster. I knew there was no point in waiting for a call, so I put on my uniform and drove to the base. Everyone met at the Security Office to get their instructions. My instructions were to take a patrol vehicle down to the South gate (a gate we only used for evacuations). I was to unlock the chain, then direct traffic to the Evac. Route. Easy enough, right? When I got there, a line of cars was already waiting to exit through the gate, so I parked, got the keys, and attempted to unlock the padlock. No luck; none of the keys seemed to work.

After screwing around for five minutes trying to get the lock to open, I heard the Watch Commander calling me on the Radio. I answered, "Base, 17, were you trying to reach me?"

"17, Base, this is Warrant Officer Bushel, why isn't your gate open yet?"

"Sir none of the keys seem to be working"

"17, base, what other options do you have? That gate must be opened."

"Sir I have but one option, I can crash the gate with my truck, and Sir, I suspect it may even help ease my frustration."

I could hear laughing in the background when he answered me, "Well Officer Troyer, if that is your only option, I give you permission to crash the gate."

"Sir yes Sir."

I got in the truck and crashed the gate. Locks and gates went flying. I calmly parked the truck and began to direct traffic. I could see the drivers laughing and shaking their heads as they drove by. From that moment on, the guys would kid around and say I was the only person on the entire base that could intentionally destroy government property and not get in trouble.

CHAPTER
17

Goats, and more.

Soon after getting to Kodiak, I went to the Personnel Office and ordered my correspondent Courses, for Petty Officer, Second class. There were certain steps I had to take to even be eligible for a promotion. First, I had to complete a year in my current rank. I also had to complete my courses for Second Class. After that I had to wait for the Coast Guard to hold a service-wide examination. This meant that on a given day, there would be an exam. Administered Service wide, all PO.3's who wished to be promoted to PO.2'S and had met all their requirements, could participate in the exam. For instance, if the Coast Guard needed 179 PO. 2's to fill slots, but 400 individuals took the test, the Coast Guard would take the scores and add points for time in service, then out of the highest scores, 179 would be promoted. Clear as mud, right?

In 1988, when I took my exam, because, the Coast Guard suddenly found themselves, overloaded with BM3's, that had, for some reason or the other stagnated, and now had 10 years or more of Service, so to help move those individuals along, they implemented a system called, (high year, ten year), this meant that if you were a BM3, with 10 years of service, you had to pass the service wide exam. and, get promoted, or get kicked out, so by putting a boot to their ass, poor little old me, with 3 years of Service, didn't stand a chance, I could have scored a 100% on my Service wide exam. and still have no chance at getting promoted, because of all those, 10, year old, BM3's. So, during my second year on Kodiak, I took the exam anyway, and just as I feared, I never even made the list. I would have to wait until the following year, then try again. Another thing that was starting to loom over my head was my enlistment was going to be up the following year, and I was expecting a phone call, any day from the West Coast detailer, telling me where I was going next. I was going to do everything in my power to convince him to let me stay in Alaska, somewhere. In the meantime, I had a Mountain Goat hunt to go on.

One should never even contemplate going on a goat hunt by themselves. Mountain Goats live in the highest, rockiest peaks. If you made just one misstep, you could fall a thousand feet down the mountain. The idea of taking a buddy is, if this should happen, he could at least tell your loved ones where they can find your carcass. Goats and sheep are considered the most difficult animals to hunt in North America. I was aware of that, so I asked some of my friends if they would consider going with me for the experience. I told them that I would pay for the float plane but couldn't afford much more than that. I wasn't too surprised when Bob White and Dale Weigand both offered to go along for the experience, and to my surprise, both insisted on paying for part of the plane.

We began to plan. My permit was for a specific unit, which was located approximately twenty-five miles down the coast of Kodiak. There were no roads, so we had to charter a float plane to take us to the base of the mountain, where we would begin a 3,000' climb up to where we hoped the goats would be.

The day of departure finally arrived. We had packed sleeping bags, light tents, freeze dried food and water. Each of our packs weighed around forty pounds. Bob had a small one-burner camp stove along to boil water for our dehydrated food, and also when we filled our drinking bottles from streams.

We packed as light as we could, with only bare essentials. We knew that the climb to the top was going to be tough, so we tried to mentally prepare ourselves as we boarded the plane. My heart was pounding with excitement as the plane began to taxi out of Kodiak Harbor. Suddenly we were airborne and the hunt was underway. It seemed like only a short time had passed when the pilot suddenly, banked a hard left, and at the same time, began his decent down to the ocean, where we landed. After taxiing to shore, we unloaded our packs, and the pilot pointed us to our mountain, then said, "Hopefully I'll see you in three days," and off he flew. After we watched the plane become just a speck in the sky, we began to slog toward the base of the mountain.

When we reached the base of the mountain and started our climb, it soon became clear this wasn't going to be an easy climb. For the first ¼ mile we fought our way through head-high weeds and Alder bushes, and it was steep. We basically used the bushes to pull ourselves up the mountain. It was extremely hard and slow going. When we eventually broke out of the bushes, it was still very steep but grassy and a lot easier to climb. Eventually, the grass began to peter out and was replaced with solid rock ledges and slopes. This terrain was actually easier to climb, although it was just as steep. Late that afternoon, we finally reached a grassy saddle. At 3,000 feet, we decided to make this our base camp, then hunt from there the next day, so we set up our tents. After we ate our dinner, we began to glass the mountains for goats. It wasn't long until we spotted a few way up in the cliffs. A couple of kids were playing and jumping from rock to rock. It was a promising sight. That night I went to sleep with high expectations for the next day.

The next morning, we were up and had our breakfast a while before daylight, then, as it began to get light, we started to move out along the saddle to an area where we could glass a number of cliffs. My tag was for either sex, and I wasn't particular, so the plan was, I would try for the first goat that didn't have kids and had legal horns. Soon after the sun began to crest, we spotted a lone goat standing on a cliff, about 300 yards away. It appeared to have about 10" horns and it didn't have any kids, so I decided to make a try for it. I stacked some rocks up for a rest, then laid my coat on top. After that, I took a careful aim and lit off a round. The first round was a hit, but it began to run toward the edge of the cliff. Just as it reached the cliff edge, my second round entered its neck, and it fell right over the cliff, toward us. It fell and rolled about 200'. When it finally came to a stop at the bottom of the cliff, it was only about 200 yards from us. I had a hard time believing I had just shot a Mountain Goat on Kodiak Island. I realized, that, for most hunters, this was a dream that would never come true for them, yet, for this young, ex-Amish lad, it had just become a reality. It certainly wasn't lost on me, just how fortunate I was.

Mountain Goat, Kodiak, Ak. 1988

After taking pictures with an old 110 Camara, we skinned and deboned it, then packed everything up and headed down the mountain. We reached the shore late that evening, where we built a fire and roasted some of the backstrap for dinner. I was amazed at how delicious it was. That night we slept with one eye open. We were camped on a beach in the heart of brown bear country. We did store the meat away from camp, but even that didn't guarantee our safety. The next morning everything was still intact, so we loaded everything on our backs once more, then hiked a mile and a half to meet the plane. Soon we heard the drone of a plane in the distance. When the pilot flew over us, he dipped his wings to let us know he saw us, then landed. When we landed in Kodiak, I split up the meat with Dale and Bob. Later I sent the hide to a Taxidermy in Anchorage, where I had it mounted.

Soon after returning from my goat hunt, Alaska experienced its worst oil spill in history, when the Tanker, Exxon Valdez, ran aground in Prince William Sound. It was the only thing on the news for weeks. Around that same time, Dale Weigand's enlistment was up, and he decided to get out and get a job on the oil spill. Exxon was throwing money around like you couldn't believe, and the word was you could make a lot of money in a short time if you went to work for them.

Dale landed a job as a deck hand on a tugboat working in the sound. Soon, word came back that he was earning a premium wage, and that there were lots of jobs to be had. I was still planning to re-enlist, but then I got my orders. I was going to Ashtabula Oh., on Lake Erie, about thirty miles from Fairport, where I had just come from. I had a decision to make. The last place I wanted to go was back where I came from. I called the detailer and tried to reason with him. I asked him to station me anywhere in Alaska. Nope, he needed me in Ashtabula.

I was devastated, I didn't know what to do, so, I asked some of the older Petty Officers for their opinion. They told me that I could get out for up to a year, then re-enlist without penalties, should I decide to. My decision was made, I would let my enlistment run out, try to get a job with Exxon, make a bit of money, then decide what to do next. The decision to get out of the service wasn't one I made lightly. I had worked my ass off to get where I was, but I also knew that having Veteran status gave me a leg up for state or government employment, and maybe I was ready to try something else. So, the Coast Guard put my belongings in storage. I had a year to decide where I wanted to have it shipped to, so I put what I needed in my car and loaded it on a ferry bound for Seward, Alaska.

Now, mind you, my intentions were to call Alaska my home. I never intended to live anywhere else, so I did some thinking on my way to Seward and decided that I was going to talk to the Chief of Police of Seward, just to see if he might be hiring anyone. I would have given up working for Exxon if I could've landed a permanent job in Seward. I unloaded my car at the dock, then went to see the Chief. I introduced myself, told him that I had just gotten out of the Coast Guard as a security Patrolman, and I was wondering if he might be hiring anyone. He swore and said he had just filled two positions two days ago with guys off the street. He said he wishes I had talked to him sooner, that he would have hired a veteran long before the two guys he just hired, and now he didn't have any openings left. I was disappointed but thanked him anyway. I wasn't worried. I decided to work for Exxon as long as I could. After that I would still have plenty of time to find a good state job. You might be wondering why I was so intent on finding a state job. Here's why: even before I joined the Coast Guard, I thought of the fact that there was a good chance that in my later years, I may not have anyone to look out for me, since none of my family would be in the picture, so I was going to try to get a job that would pay a retirement pension. I saw it as a safety net for my future.

I had in my car an old down sleeping bag from the Korean war era that someone had given me, and a small, cheap piece of crap tent. I had put all my guns in storage, probably a mistake. Anyway, that first night I made it as far as Eagle River, a small Community East of Anchorage. I didn't want to spend money on a motel, so I parked along a back road and set up my tent. After rolling out my sleeping bag, I went to sleep. Sometime during the night, it began to rain. By five am, I woke up, lying in 4" of water, my down sleeping bag soaked up all the water it could, and I soaked up the rest. I could barely lug that heavy sleeping bag back to my car. I threw it and the tent into the first dumpster I found, then I went back to the Airforce Base to the Commissary, where I bought a better sleeping bag and a .22 cal. Semiautomatic pistol. I began to feel much better as I drove on to Valdez.

I rolled into Valdez late that afternoon, and, as I approached the town I noticed what looked like tent cities spread out along the road. Wherever there was a flat spot, the closer I got to town, the worse it got. There were makeshift tarps and tents set up in every yard. I could hardly drive through the street, there were so many people. I stopped at a motel to see about a room,. They laughed at me and said Exxon had rented every motel in town for the unforeseeable future, and they were paying 300.00 dollars per room, per night. They also said that the locals were even renting their lawns to the tent people for 75.00 per night, and they were getting 150.00 per night for a space inside their homes to put a sleeping bag.

Well, now what? Since there were no rooms, how about a job? While driving around town, I spotted a security guard standing in front of a building, so I stopped and asked him who I needed to talk to about a job. He told me to talk to his boss, he told me to follow him, so I followed him inside the building, where he introduced his boss to me. I told him who I was, and that I had just been released from the Coast Guard and was looking for a job. He said that every morning 100 or more people would line up in front of the Exxon Headquarters at 7:00, then Exxon would read off around twenty names of people they would hire. The rest of the people would have to come back every morning in the hopes that their name would be called. He said it can take a week or more to get hired for the actual cleanup, but he said that he may have an opening in a few days for a Security Guard. He said he would pay 12.00 per hour plus overtime for shore duty and 16.00 per hour plus overtime for ship duty. Now, that was a lot of money for 1989.

I asked him what I should do next. He said, "Go sleep in your car until you get hired. After that, we will feed and house you." I told him that sounded good, and that I would see him at 7:00 am.

That afternoon I headed out of town to find a safe place to park my car and get some sleep. I finally found a rather secluded little road that looked promising. As I followed it, it suddenly dead-ended at an abandoned bridge, crossing a glacial stream. This looked like a good, out of the way place, so I crawled into my sleeping bag in the front seat and fell wide awake.

That night, I began to second guess my choices. It dawned on me that at that moment, I was officially homeless and jobless. I lay awake thinking about my father and the rest of my family, and although I had written letters to them, I found myself longing to see them again. It was then I decided, if I get a job on the oil spill, I would work until fall, then go to Pa. for the winter, but first thing in the spring, I would return to Alaska and make it my home. After that I must have fallen asleep. The annoying sound of an alarm got me awake. It took me a minute to figure out where I was, and what the heck I was doing sleeping in my car. Suddenly it came to me. I have to be in town by 0700. I rooted through my junk until I found my toothbrush and deodorant, then I crawled down the riverbank and brushed my teeth, and cleaned up as best I could. Good Heavens, that water was cold! After repacking my things, I drove the fourteen miles into town, just to be told no job yet, come back tomorrow. Finally, on the fourth morning, I was hired by Purcell Securities. I would be guarding a gate entrance to one of Exxon's man camps. I would be working night shift, twelve hours on, twelve off, seven days a week. When my shift ended, I would stay at a man camp and eat at the food camp. Exxon had hired real chefs. They kept a buffet going 24-7, and the food was excellent. After working in Valdez, for two weeks, my boss asked me if I would like to work on a ship. My wage, would increase to 16.00 per hour, and I would be working fifteen hour days, seven days per week. My new job would be to go to shore with the cleanup crew every morning, then I was to watch the beach for bears. If I saw one, I was to get everyone back on the boat. Other than that, there was nothing else for me to do. I told him I would love to go.

The following morning, I found a relatively safe place to park my car, then I boarded a shuttle boat that took a bunch of us out to the boat where I would spend the next six weeks. I did basically nothing the entire time I worked for Exxon. It was by far the most boring job I ever hoped to have, the only thing that kept me there being the fact that I was making more money then I had ever dreamed of making. I knew that this was going to be a real boost to my economy, and to top it off, there was nowhere to spend my money, so I just watched it increase.

Sleeping quarters on the ship were extremely tight. There were six bunk beds, three per side, in a room no more than 8' by 8'. There was a narrow little floor space, just big enough for two people to stand upright, so we had to take turns going to bed and getting up. It was more like going to your coffin every night. In the morning we got up, ate breakfast at the buffet, then walked down a 30' narrow hallway, lined on both sides with pallets, filled with all sorts of drinks and snacks. While walking, we filled a bag with whatever food we needed for that day. At the end of the hallway was our waiting landing craft, ready to take us to shore for the next fifteen hours. At the end of the day, we would return to the ship, eat dinner, get a shower, go to bed. The next day, same thing all over again.

Onboard ship, working for Exxon,

I kept thinking about Dale Weigand. I knew he was a deckhand on a tug boat attached to a barge, somewhere in the Prince William Sound. Now, Prince William Sound is huge, so he could be miles from me, I really didn't know where he could be. There was a shuttle/messenger boat that traveled between all the ships. It was primarily used to shuttle Exxon big wigs from boat to boat. I asked the captain if he would try to locate Dale on one of the Barges, and if he finds him, I asked that he tell Dale where I was. He said he would be happy to. A few days later when he returned, he said that he had found Dale. He said he was about ninety miles from where I was. He also said that Dale sent a message for me: that I should try to get transferred to his barge, if I could. I thanked the captain for the information. Later I asked my supervisor if getting transferred would be a possibility. He said sure, if there's an opening. He said he would make a phone call. The next day, my supervisor told me he had secured a spot for me on Dale's Barge, but I would have to get my car in Valdez, then drive 400 miles back through Anchorage, then down the Seward Highway to a small Coastal town called Whittier. The only way to get to Whittier was by boat or rail. Then once I arrive at Whittier, I would park my car and catch a shuttle boat out to the Barge. I told him I would go, so, that afternoon, I caught a shuttle to Valdez.

After getting my car and hitting the road, I thought how good it felt to be out of those cramped quarters. I enjoyed the drive to the railyard below Anchorage. There I bought a ticket for my car to be hauled to Whittier. Soon they motioned for me to drive my car onto a rail car. I was instructed to remain in my car until we arrived. After a twenty-minute ride, we arrived, I unloaded and parked, grabbed my belongings, then boarded the shuttle boat. The ride to the barge was about three hours long, and cold. When we arrived I was amazed that the barge was 600' long, the one end had berthing and office containers, where a bunch of Exxon Executives stayed and worked. I stayed in a small room, in a container. I liked it much better than the tight sleeping quarters I had just come from. Tethered to the side of the Barge was a 110' tugboat assigned to the barge. That is where Dale was staying, since he was a deck hand, on the Tug. I went over to the Tug and yelled for Dale. It was good to see a familiar face again, so we talked for a while until it was time to get to work.

There was only two Security Guards on board, me and one other guy. Our job was to stand twelve-hour shifts, behind a desk, at the barge entrance. My orders were to check every person that came and went, to make sure they were authorized to be there, and anyone who came back to the barge from town was to have their bags searched for alcohol, since no alcohol was allowed. Late one night an Exxon person coming back from town, tried to sneak past me, so I called out to him to come back to me so I could check him in. He called me all kinds of names as he came up to my post. After finding his name on my list, I told him that I would have to check his bag. He started cussing and carrying on and refused to let me check it. I had been nothing but polite to him. It didn't seem to matter, he stormed up to the office, and soon I was summoned up to the office for a phone call. It was from my supervisor on the ship I had left. He asked me what had transpired. I told him that I was just trying to do my job, and the guy went off on me. He was totally understanding, but told me that from now on, I should just stand at my post and do nothing, because apparently the executives don't want to follow their own rules. I told him that I understood and went back to my post.

Now, I have always tried to do any job assigned to me to the best of my ability, and I don't mind being chastised if I screw up, but I do not like being yelled at if I didn't do anything wrong, maybe a possible holdover, from when I was Amish, when the bishops, would chastise me for something I didn't do. The following morning, when I saw Dale, I was still feeling the sting, so, I took that opportunity to vent to him. He completely understood and said that his captain would probably hire me if I wanted to work as a deckhand on the tug. I told him I would be interested, if the Captain would have me. Later that day the Captain had me fill out an application, and an hour later I was a deck hand, living on the tug. I actually got a pay raise to 22.00 per hour, and Dale and I were working together again.

I liked my new job, it was hard work, but I enjoyed it. was almost the end of October now, and the weather was changing fast, ice was beginning to form in some spots, and the word from Exxon was that the clean-up operation would be put on hold soon for the winter. They also began to fire people for the smallest offences, it seemed. The rumor was that the more people they could fire, the fewer people would be collecting unemployment from them.

I figured, since I was the last hire on the tug, that I would be the first to go when they decided to slim down the crew for the winter.

I didn't really mind, since I planned to go home for the winter anyway. A few days later, the captain told us that we would be securing everything on the barge in preparation for towing across the Gulf of Alaska to the town of Seward, where the barge would be moored for the winter. After a day of lashing everything down, the tug was hooked to the barge. The tug had a roll of steel cable mounted on the aft deck, pointed astern, the cable was then hooked to the 600' Barge, and the captain ordered several hundred yards of cable be fed out.

After that, the barge began to follow us into the Gulf. While the captain was doing this, Dale and I cooked supper for everyone. After everyone finished eating, I cleaned up, then went out on deck to help Dale with the cable, since the captain was now on the right heading for Seward. He ordered a half mile of cable be let out. After we did that, he asked Dale to come to the bridge, where he gave Dale the heading and the helm. After that he went to his cabin for the night. I sat on the bridge with Dale, and we talked about old times on Kodiak and what our future plans were. He was going to try to stay on the tug for as long as he could. I told him about my plans to go home for the winter, then come back to Alaska to live. We talked for most of the night. It was a pleasant but rough voyage across the Gulf, and one I will never forget.

NOTE: Dale stayed on the tug until he earned his Captain's license, then he ran a tug in Southeast Alaska for a number of years, until he moved back to Sturgeon Bay, Wisconsin, where he continues to work as a tugboat Captain to this Day. NOTE: As for the rest of my Kodiak friends. Bob White and Lemert Roberson both retired from the Coast Guard and never left Kodiak. They live there to this day. Tim Mauldin got out of the Coast Guard and returned home to North Carolina, where he worked at a Water Treatment Plant, and in his words, "I waded through enough crap to eventually become the plant Superintendent." Tim has since retired. My own story continues.

CHAPTER
18

Going Home

As we moored the 600' barge to the Seward docks, my mind was in turmoil, I was experiencing conflicting emotions, part of me didn't want to leave Alaska, and the other part of me, longed to see my dad, whom I had not seen in over two years. In the end, family won the battle, and I informed the captain that I would be leaving the tug and going home for the winter. He wished me well, then he arranged a ride for me on a Linden Corporation truck as far as the Whittier railyard, so I could pick up my car. I said goodbye to Dale as I climbed into the passenger seat, then, after a one hour ride, I caught the train into Whittier and retrieved my car.

That afternoon, as I hit the road toward Canada and home, I thought about all that had transpired over the last four and a half, years, and especially over the last two and a half years in Alaska. I really felt that I had lived more of a life in the past four and a half years than I would have lived in a lifetime of living Amish. Later that evening, as I approached the Canadian border, a weird feeling began to creep into my head. What if this was it? What if, for some reason, I wouldn't be able to return in the spring, as planned? I tried to shake the feeling out of my head but couldn't, and as I looked at the Welcome to Alaska sign in my rearview mirror, my emotions got the best of me and tears began to flow from my eyes, and at that moment, I couldn't help but wonder if Alaska would ever really be my home again.

As I continued along the Alcan Highway, down through British Columbia, I was awestruck by the beauty of the Canadian Rockies. I really enjoyed the drive, at least until I re-entered the United States in Seattle, Washington. I was no longer accustomed to the traffic and chaos of the lower forty-eight. As soon as I left Seattle, the landscape began to open up, and the drive became enjoyable again. It was late September 1989, fall was in the air, the Western Aspen trees had turned to a bright yellow and were in stark contrast to the bright green pines, it was a very beautiful time of year for traveling, the mountain tops were covered with a light coating of snow, and, at that moment, I began to miss Alaska with all my heart.

I took my time traveling through the western states. I stopped to see some of the attractions that I missed on my way out, two and a half years prior, such as the Devils tower, the black hills, and several museums along the way. Later, as I approached Chicago, I remembered why I held zero fondness for the Eastern U.S.

To this day, I don't understand how anyone could have thought that it would be a good idea, to build a large, congested city, strategically placed up against a lake, making it virtually impossible to go east or west without traveling through it. I'm thinking, the Cow that kicked over the lantern that caused Chicago to burn flat to the ground definitely had the right idea. Where is a Cow when I need one? Ten hours after passing through Chicago, I arrived at my sister Mary and her husband's place. It was good to see them again, and we sure had a lot to talk about. The next day, I went to see Dad and my brothers. They seemed happy to see me, which was nice. I was a little shocked to learn that my family had been land shopping in Ohio, with plans to possibly move out there within a year, and as a result, the Amish church where I grew up, would be dissolved, and now that I was out of the Coast Guard, my brothers began to apply a little pressure on me to come back to the Amish, and move out there with them, but after I told them, that, the likelihood of that happening, was less than, zero, they quit asking me.

After my return to Pa., I began to hunt around for a place to rent for the winter. I also put the word out that I was looking for a part time job to hold me over winter. It wasn't long until I found an old farmhouse for rent, about two miles from Dad's place. It seemed to fit the bill, so I moved in. It felt good to have my own place. It was out in the countryside, and very quiet. A few days later the lady at the local country store told me that her brother-in-law, Roger Hess, was starting a new business recycling tires, and that he might be looking to hire someone. I wasn't particular what kind of work I would be doing, I just wanted a little income, so as not to deplete my savings. Earlier, I had found a nice Toyota pick-up at a used car lot. I had been keeping my eyes open for a pick-up for a while now, so when I found this one, it seemed to be exactly what I was looking for. After striking a deal, I traded my car in. On the pick-up, I actually paid very little out of pocket, so I felt pretty good about that. I now needed a name for my new Jitney, so I plastered *The Lone Wolf* on the bug shield. Now it was complete.

I was pretty much settled into my rental, so I decided to go see Mr. Roger Hess about a job. I knew of Roger most of my life. He and his wife, Leona, farmed a lot of land along the Susquehanna River. They farmed many acres of tomatoes and strawberries, along with other crops. My siblings picked tomatoes for them in the early years, and that is why the name was familiar. They were always associated with farming though, so I didn't quite know what to expect. When I heard they were starting a new business, recycling scrap tires, I was curious and I needed work, so I drove over one morning to talk to them. I met Roger as soon as I arrived. After I introduced myself, I told him that I heard he might be hiring, and that I was looking for a job for the winter. He asked me who my dad was. When I told him, he said that he baled hay for him years ago, and he thought he remembered me as a child. After that, he said he would hire me, then he asked if I could start the next morning. I told him I could. Before I left, he introduced his eighteen-year-old son Troy to me and said that I would be working with him most of the time. I was excited to start my new job. That evening I packed a lunch for the next day, then set my alarm. Work was to start at 0700, and I wanted to be there a little early.

The next morning when I got to work, Troy and his dad came out of the house to greet me, and at that time Roger gave us our marching orders for that day, then he left for the day. As soon as he was gone, Troy told me to come into the house. He wanted to show me something. When we got inside, Troy began to show me a bunch of trophies he had earned throwing discus, then he told me that he had won States just recently. Now, I had no idea what a Discus was, and I hadn't even heard of anyone earning a trophy for throwing a piece of metal just a little farther then someone else, this coupled with the fact that Roger had given us things to do that day, and standing around in the house listening to an eighteen-year-old boy telling me about his trophies certainly wasn't what he had told us to do, I felt nervous and out of place. If I learned anything in the military, it was that when you were given orders, you followed them, and without question. I wasn't the gushing kind, and I simply couldn't muster any enthusiasm for something I didn't understand anyway, so I told Troy that we should probably get to work. He looked a little offended, but we went outside and started working. Sometime during that first day, I had the pleasure of meeting Troy's older brother Todd. I never got to work with him much, because he spent most of his time driving tractor trailer. He did help with the farming when he wasn't driving,

There was a horse barn just out from the house. Often when I walked past it, I would glance in at the horses. Not that I cared much for horses—I had my fill of them—but they weren't bad looking horses, and it was obvious that someone was taking care of them. One evening Troy and I were walking past the horse barn when suddenly out of the corner of my eye, I saw a young girl standing there.

At the same time, Troy asked if I had met his sister Denise. I said no! In my mind I was thinking, *I didn't even know you had sister.*

We were introduced, she smiled at me shyly and blushed, I smiled at her, and thought, wow! She looks like a nice country girl, then we went about our business for the rest of the day, after that I couldn't get her out of my mind. After a few days, I finally ask Troy, in my most casual voice, if Denise had a boyfriend. He said she didn't, then he looked at me and asked, "Do you want me to ask her out for you? I said, "No I don't." I thought something as important as that shouldn't be farmed out to an eighteen-year-old, so that evening, I went to my house and thought about it. What if she says yes, and I like her, what becomes of Alaska in the spring?

I finally came up with the rationale that she probably wouldn't say yes, anyway, and even if she did accept, what could one date hurt? So, I called their house, the phone rang, then someone picked up. I asked if Denise was there. The person said, I'll get her."

Soon a girl answered. I told her who I was and asked if she would like to go to dinner with me. After a short pause, she said, "Yes I would."

I said, "How about Saturday, around 6pm?"

She was ok with that, so we hung up. The following day was Saturday, so I went and got a haircut and washed my truck. After that, I called a restaurant and made reservations. Later that evening, I dressed in my best going out clothes, then drove to their house and went inside. When she finally came down the stairs, we left on our first date.

That evening of our first date, we were both a little shy at first, then, during our meal we started to talk like old friends. She told me that the reason I never saw her around was because she worked construction as a flag person, and she left for work early and came home late. I was intrigued.

Afterwards we went to see a movie. By the time I dropped her off at her house, I knew that I wanted to go out again, so, before she got out of the truck, I asked her if she wanted to go out again, and, to my surprise, she said yes. Right then, I began to think that she might be the one I was looking for. She seemed kind and caring, she was fun to be around, but still shy enough to blush at almost everything, I was starting to fall in love, and I wasn't sure how to handle it. I spent the next couple of days thinking how this might affect my future. I was sure that if we started dating steady, Alaska in the spring, or even in the next couple of years, might be out of the question. I decided to let the chips fall where they may, for the time being. I wasn't that old yet, so I figured I would have at least a couple of years to figure things out.

I had been working for Roger about two and a half months now, and Denise and I had been dating steady for about a month. We were getting along really well, and even mused, about what our future might hold, now and then. I would have had to be blind not to notice that the rest of the family wasn't as keen about us dating as we were, for whatever reason. They didn't seem to care much for me, and that resulted in me being a little uncomfortable when I was around them, so I told Denise that I would try to find another job. She had been getting some pressure from her family to break up with me, so she agreed that I would probably be happier working somewhere else, and maybe her family wouldn't pressure her as much if I didn't work there every day.

The state penitentiary in Camphill Pa. had just experienced one of the worst inmate riots in history, and, as a result, many of the guards had been injured. Others had quit, either out of fear or frustration, so the state was hiring guards to backfill the openings. When I heard this, I took a day off work so I could take the Civil Service Exam for Correctional Officer. After passing the exam, I was scheduled for an interview, sometime later. In the meantime, I approached Roger and thanked him for giving me employment, then I gave him my two-week notice. I thought. I noticed some hostility when he said, "I don't need two weeks' notice. You can leave now." So I did.

A few weeks before even applying for the prison job, I had applied and been accepted for a Deputy Wildlife Conservation Officer position (which was later officially changed to Deputy Game Warden), so, for convenience sake, I will refer to it as such. The Deputy Game Warden position is a part-time position with full law-enforcement powers, but work under an assigned Game Warden. Once a person is accepted as a Deputy, you attend a week-long academy, where you are taught the policies and procedures of Wildlife law-enforcement, along with weapons qualifications and self-defense tactics. Then, after graduating, you work with another person until you are deemed fully qualified. Only after all that are you free to work by yourself. My academy date wasn't for another couple of months, and I knew that if the prison would hire me, there would probably be some kind of conflict with the dates that I would have to deal with.

Deputy Game Warden, 1990

It wasn't long until I received a notice from the Department of Corrections to appear for an interview. When I walked into the room, there were maybe fifteen other people sitting there. I found an empty chair beside a fellow about my age. He introduced himself as Scott Lightner. I told him who I was, and we talked for a while until the Corrections Personnel entered the room. One of them asked if all the veterans would raise their hands. I looked around, and everyone had raised their hands, then the lady said, "All of you are hired." Scott looked at me and said, "Is that it?" I said, "I guess!"

We spent the next hour filling out paperwork and getting our dates for the Correctional Academy, which was two weeks at a nearby office complex. We were also asked if we had any unfinished business that might interfere with our training, and if so, now would be the time to get it documented, since we weren't authorized to take any leave for at least six months, so I had them document the dates for my Game Warden Academy, which they did.

The following Monday, we reported to the Correctional Officer Academy, to begin our two weeks of intensive training. Scott and I sat close to each other. The entire two weeks, we talked during every break. It was during those two weeks that we started a friendship that lasted for thirty-two years until his untimely death in January 2022. He will be missed.

CHAPTER
19

Sniper Training

After graduation from the Correctional Academy, we were assigned our shifts. As CO Apprentices, we were required to work a one week rotation through all three shifts, then after six months, if all our training manuals were filled out and signed by our training Sgt., we would be promoted to a CO1. After that, we could bid for a position, according to seniority.

Normally we would not be allowed to take leave during the first year, and certainly not during our six months of training. However, my Game Warden Academy date fell right in the middle of my six months training. In the meantime, I was keeping my training Sgt. in the loop, and he was also aware that my leave had been approved by the Prison Warden. During my hiring process, he suggested that I still submit a request for leave, just for the record, so that is what I did. It turns out, the Lieutenant in charge of leave requests apparently wasn't aware that my leave had already been approved, so he disapproved it. I, of course, didn't know that he had disapproved it, so I went to my academy for a week, where I endured even more intensive training. Then, at the end of a week, we raised our right hands and were sworn in as Deputy Game Wardens.

Immediately, after returning to the prison, I was summoned to the Lt's office, where I was informed that I was going to be fired for being AWOL for a week during my apprenticeship. But since I was no longer an un-informed, young Amish lad, but a veteran with some life experience, not to mention a recently sworn-in Deputy Game Warden, I looked the Lt. right in the eye, and told him that I didn't think so, since my leave was approved by the prison's Warden even before I was hired.

He began shuffling papers, as his face turned crimson. Finally he said I have to have proof. I told him he could ask my training Sgt. for a copy, then I returned to my cell block. After my six months were up and my checkoffs were completed, I was promoted to a CO1. Within my first year, I became a member of the Corrections Emergency Response Team, also known as the CERT team. We were the first to respond to any inmate disturbances, and we were responsible for performing cell searches and inmate extractions from their cells if they refused to come out. Basically, if there was trouble, we were the folks that responded. After a year and a half of working at the prison, I applied for the Prison Sniper Program.

My thinking was that if there was another riot, I would take my chances up on a rooftop, with a sniper rifle. The program was new, so I became one of the first thirty people trained as snipers, state-wide. The sniper school was an intensive, two-week long program, where we were taught the formulas and trigonometry necessary to adjust our optics for a consistent, one shot, one kill. During the final exam, before graduation, we placed our weapons on the ground, then we sprinted for a quarter of a mile to get our heart rate up. After we returned to our rifles, we dropped down and placed three rounds into a 2"X4" rectangular square at 300 yards in less than a minute. We were only given three rounds, we couldn't have any misses, and to remain sniper qualified, we had to do this every three months. I truly enjoyed sniper school.

Denise and I had been dating for about a year now, so I worked up the nerve to ask her to marry me. I was thrilled when she said yes. Later, we decided on March 2nd, 1991, as our wedding day. In the meantime, my brothers had purchased land in Ohio, where they planned to start a new Amish settlement, so, to get the most for their land here in Pa. three of them decided to sub-divide several lots off of their original farms.

My brother Sam then built a nice, three-bedroom log house on one of his lots. Denise and I decided that we would really like to buy it as our first house. I knew I couldn't buy it, because I was shunned, but since we weren't married yet, Denise decided she would buy it, so she approached Sam, and a deal was made. After the sale was final, Denise insisted that I move into her house. Actually, while I was working at the prison one day, she moved me into her house. I was also interested in a four-acre adjoining lot that Sam had listed in real estate, and since it was listed in real estate, he couldn't really control who bought it, so I was able to purchase it with money I had saved from the oil spill, so now we had a total of 7 ½ acres, with a new house. We felt very fortunate.

I stayed very busy during that time, working at the prison, then patrolling as a Game Warden, evenings and weekends. I must say though, working as a Game Warden was by far the most enjoyable law enforcement work I had ever done.

I always had a love for Wildlife, and the outdoors, so this was a great opportunity to try to make a difference, but not only that, it was fun. During the winter, when the hunting seasons were in, we were kept busy investigating hunting violations, but during the summer, when it became a little quieter, except for parties in the Game land parking lots, this occurred almost every weekend, normally lots of litter would be left behind, and on top of that, people, would often throw their garbage out in the parking lots, and elsewhere on the game lands. To try to discourage folks from dumping their garbage out, I would spend hours, if need be, rooting through garbage bags, trying to find something, with a name and an address on it. It was hard to believe how often people would leave their empty prescription pill bottles or envelopes in their garbage for me to find. The hardest dumping violation to find evidence in were the ashes from a burn barrel, but that didn't stop me from trying. There is almost always some part of a magazine that doesn't quite burn up, and several times, I got lucky enough to find an address, which resulted in the perpetrator becoming unlucky.

Going back to the parties in the parking lots, we would take a different approach to that. We would hide our vehicle a short distance from the parking lot, generally before dark, on a Friday or Saturday, then we would hide in the bushes adjacent to the parking lot, and wait for someone to arrive.

There were no guarantees that anyone would arrive, but more times than not, one or two vehicles would show up at some point. Often they would start a bonfire, which was illegal, or they would start drinking beer, which was illegal while on State Game Lands. Now, rather than taking their empty beer cans or bottles, with them, they would start throwing them into the bushes, the same bushes we were hiding in. Since we had no idea which direction they would be throwing the next bottle, we had to stay on our toes. There were some very close calls at times. We would take mental notes of who threw what, and where, then, after a sufficient number of bottles had gone sailing into the brush, we would walk out and introduce ourselves as State Game Wardens. One Deputy would control the remaining beer, for evidence, while the other Deputy would retrieve several bottles from the bushes. The perpetrators almost always denied throwing any bottles, until we showed them that the batch numbers on the bottles matched the batch number on their case of beer. After issuing the appropriate citations, we would set them free, as long as one of them was fit to drive. By using tactics like these, we weren't able to stop littering, but felt we were slowing it down. I continued to serve as a Deputy Game Warden for nearly nine years. Finally, when Denise began to worry about me working alone at night, I decided, for her peace of mind, to hang it up.

A while before moving to Denise's house, I had noticed that my landlord, was wearing a Masons Ring, so I asked him what it was all about. He explained that it was an organization that strived to make good men better, and they were also involved with the Shriners Hospital, along with many charities across the world. I thought it sounded interesting, so I asked him how I could become a Free Mason. He brought me an application to fill out, then he and another Mason signed and submitted it to the Blue Lodge for acceptance. After it was approved by the lodge, I went through all the required steps and was raised to a Master Mason. This was in 1991. Thirty years later, I am still a member, and have never even considered resigning.

Our wedding day was fast approaching. I had been living at Denise's house, alone, for a while now, so I was looking forward to us getting married, so we could move in together and start our life as a couple. Prior to our wedding, I had asked Denise if she thought moving to Alaska was a possibility. She said she had always dreamed of living in Alaska, so she didn't see any reason why we shouldn't. I was willing to wait a few years, if necessary, but I didn't want to wait too long. I wanted to start a career up there, while I was still young enough to succeed.

The day of our wedding finally arrived. It was a beautiful wedding. We had arranged to have it at a local church, Denise had taken charge of all the details, my job was to show up, look handsome, and say, I DO, which I did. There were a lot of guests. All but two were Denise's friends and family. The two that weren't were my sister Lydia and her husband George. I was so happy they could make it. After the reception, we left for Louisiana on our Honeymoon. Neither one of us had ever been to Louisiana. We decided it would be nice to see what the deep South was all about. We ate where the locals ate, and we tried very hard to avoid tourist traps. We wanted to experience Louisiana for what it was. We sure had an enjoyable time.

After we returned home from our honeymoon, we moved Denise's belongings into our house, then we returned to our jobs. After that, we began a romantic and happy life together— NOT SO FAST. We were both a bit strong willed, so, for the first three years of our marriage, we definitely had our share of disagreements. Some of them were quite heated at times. I wanted us to be a family, and make our own decisions, but Denise had a hard time, letting go of her family, and, in her dad's eyes, I couldn't do anything right it seemed. Almost every decision I made, he would try to convince her that it was a dumb decision. In short, I ended up fighting two fronts it seemed. Fortunately, for us, after a few years, Denise began to see what was going on, and decided she would try to ignore the interference. Only after that were we able to become a cohesive couple, and slowly, we started to become attached to one another. It was fortunate that we both agreed divorce wasn't an option, so, for that reason, we were able to stick it out.

While we were living at our log house, Roger asked Denise to come work for him at the new tire recycling plant. She asked me what I thought. I told her that she would have to make that decision, and I reminded her what it was like working for family, but she decided to do it anyway. I would continue to work at the jail until 1993.

We had been living at our first house for a year now, when an older lady that Denise knew very well decided she wanted to sell her eight-five acre farm in Juniata Co. She told Denise she wanted $85,000, for it. We talked about it and decided that it would be nice to have more land. Now the house was an old farmhous, sitting on a stone foundation, full of holes, the rest of the house was in terrible shape and barely livable, full of snake skins and Squirrel skeletons. Everything about it was hideous, the barn was literally irreparable. I saw potential in the house, with a lot of work, but the barn would have to be replaced sometime. The great thing was all the land. I was intrigued, so we put our house up for sale, and within a week it was sold. Later, we sold our four-acre lot as well.

We were able to get a loan for the farm based on our equity, and instead of getting a thirty-year mortgage, we decided to tighten our belts and go for a fifteen-year mortgage instead. Neither one of us wanted to be in debt longer than we had to. When we sold our house, we had forty-five days to vacate, so, when we bought the farm, we gave the tenant thirty days to get out. Both dates were dangerously close together. We ended up moving our things in one door, and at the same time, moving the tenant out the other door. That first night Denise didn't sleep much. There was a hole in the ceiling right above our bed, and she was afraid a snake might fall down on top of us. Needless to say we slept with the lights on all night.

I patched holes throughout the house to try to make it livable. As I began to remodel, one room at a time, evenings and weekends, it took a total of ten years to complete it. The following winter, we had a rough winter and the old barn finally collapsed under a load of snow. The rest of that winter I cleaned up the mess, I burned up the entire barn on a bonfire. The following spring, we wanted to rebuild the barn but didn't have the money, so I talked to a logger about cutting the timber in our woods. We used that money to rebuild the barn.

I had a forty-five minute drive to the prison every day. I liked to work there, but I wasn't crazy about the drive, so when I heard that there was an opening with the Game Commissions, (Food and Cover Core), Denise and I agreed that since my workplace would only be five miles from our house, I should apply for the position. Working for food and cover was still a state job, so my retirement and medical, plus my years of service, would transfer over. I would get paid less per hour, but we figured that the fuel I would save would eventually pay for itself, so I applied and was eventually hired. So, after working at the penitentiary for three years, I made a lateral transfer to the Game Commission, a move I have never regretted.

CHAPTER

20

9-11-2001

My first day in my new Job with the Game Commission was spent learning our areas of responsibility and the type of work I would be doing. Everything was considered on the job training, and there were tasks that had to be mastered in order to be promoted to a Game Lands Maintenance worker II. I started out as a one but was told that as soon as I acquired the necessary skills and knowledge, I could be promoted to a worker two. Our area included six game lands over three counties. It was over 15,000, acres total. We were only a three-man crew, one of which was the supervisor. His boss was a Game Warden, also known as a Land Manager. He was in charge of three crews like ours, all in different areas, so we only saw him maybe twice a week, the rest of the time we just did what we knew had to be done. We were responsible for maintaining the parking lots, all roads, signage, boundary lines, etc. In other words, anything that resembled maintenance. Our equipment consisted of tractors, dozers, chainsaws, etc. the job was low stress, hands-on physical labor, small crew. It soon became clear to me, this was exactly the type of job I was looking for.

We had been married now for about three years, and I still hadn't given up my dream of living in Alaska. In fact, I had been trying to convince Denise that we should go sooner than later. Denise is the type of person who needs encouragement, or at the very least approval, from her family when it comes to something this monumental, so, every time she would mention moving to them, she would get nothing but a barrage of discouragement, even ridicule. This began to frustrate me to no end. I simply couldn't make any progress with that type of interference.

By now, I had saved up almost three weeks of leave, so I told Denise we should take a vacation to Alaska. She was totally in agreement, so in 1994, I took her to Alaska. We flew to Anchorage, then over to Kodiak, where we visited Lennart and Heidi. After that, we took the ferry boat back over to Seward, where we rode the train back to Anchorage. There we rented a minivan, and for the next week, we drove around Alaska. Denise seemed to really enjoy herself, but I still wasn't able to get a commitment from her to actually move there.

Shortly after returning home, Denise was excitedly telling her family how beautiful Alaska was and how much fun we had on vacation. She was so disappointed at her family's reaction. It seemed like they were afraid that if they showed any interest, she might be encouraged to move, so they showed a mild interest, at best, then brushed it aside. Not even an ounce of encouragement was offered, which I felt was unfortunate. I have always felt that encouraging your children to try new things is an important aspect in life. Apparently not all parents felt that way.

During the first ten years of our marriage, we had many discussions about moving to Alaska. Most of them ended in arguments and frustration. Finally, after about ten years, I gave up trying. I felt I had too much time invested in my career with the Game Commission to just walk away. We did, however, continue to take our vacations in Alaska every two to three years.

Shortly after returning home from Alaska in 1989, my dad and four brothers moved to Somerset, Ohio, to start a new Amish settlement. Dad's church in Snyder County had recently gone through a split, when more than half of the families decided they'd had enough of the Old Order Amish lifestyle, so they left and joined various higher Mennonite churches. This split had a devastating effect on the already small community. Hardly anyone was left, other than my dad and brothers.

Dad was the bishop and had a reputation as a bit of a hardliner, so when there was obvious sin being tolerated among some churches, he felt compelled to call it out. Dad was tormented by the fact that some of the higher, more sophisticated churches in Juniata and Lancaster Co. along with a few others, scattered about, allowed bed courtship, where young folks, while dating, were allowed to get in a bed together, which, more often than not would result in pre-marital sex, a clear violation of the Scriptures.

Most of the Amish churches, including, the ones I was associated with in my youth, wouldn't have dreamed of allowing this heinous act in their churches. In fact, if you would have even dreamed of dating in a bed, you would have been banned until you truly confessed your sins and expressed true contrition for at least six months.

Dad was convinced that if the churches that didn't allow bed courtship would just band together and stop associating with the churches that allowed it, the applied pressure may convince them to try to eradicate this obvious sin that has plagued some so called-Amish churches for many years. So, sometime later, at a large bishops meeting, Dad asked if anyone would be willing to stand with him on this idea.

Only, one or two bishops pledged to stand with him. All the others, including the Norfolk, Prattsburgh, and Clyde, N.Y., churches (the same ones that harassed me during my youth for minor infractions), decided they would rather go along to get along than stand up against sin. They also warned Dad that if he didn't drop this divisive idea, they would stop associating with him. Of course, Dad didn't give it up, so all the Amish churches, with the exception of one or two small settlements, disassociated themselves from him. This meant he could no longer preach at any of the Amish churches, and they wouldn't recognize his church as being legitimate. And, just like that, for standing against sin, Dad and my brothers found themselves standing alone, so they moved to Ohio in the hopes that like-minded families might join them. Only one did.

While Dad and my brothers lived in Ohio, Denise and I would travel out to visit them at least several times a year. Dad would always ask about his old English friends back in Snyder Co. He often said how he missed those Snyder Co. hills.

Dad was getting older. I could tell his health was slowly fading. After all, he was in his 80's. Then, late one afternoon, one of my brothers called to tell us that dad had taken a turn for the worse, and that if we wanted to see him, we should come out to Ohio as soon as possible. That same afternoon we drove to his place. We arrived around midnight. The family was gathered in the dimly lit living room. Dad was lying on a makeshift bed in the middle of the room. As soon as I walked in, he looked at me and, in a weak voice, said, "There is my baby."

I felt the tears welling in my eyes. As I held his hand, all my childhood memories rushed to my head, and my love for my dad could not have been greater than it was at that moment. He tried to comfort me, as I quietly sat by his side, with tears trickling down my face.

By some miracle, the next morning he was a little stronger and was able to sit in his rocker. Denise and I stayed by his side for a few days, as he slowly regained some of his strength back. When he appeared some-what stable, we decided to go back home, but, before we left, Dad reached for his bible. After turning to the book of Romans, chapter thirteen, he said that he could not condone my choice of lifestyle, however, since I had joined the military and was now a Deputy Game Warden, he felt that, according to Romans thirteen, I was sanctioned by God as one of God's Ministers, to bring Wrath to the evildoers. Then with tears in his eyes, he asked me a simple question, "So if God sanctions you, what right do I have to condemn you?"

I couldn't speak. I simply held his hands for a long time. Finally, he whispered goodbye. I squeezed his hands and looked at him through tear-filled eyes. At that moment, we both knew this would be the last time we would see each other alive, on this earth.

We returned home that same afternoon. We were both sad because we knew that any day we would probably be returning to Ohio. Several days later, on September 13th, 1997, we received the dreaded phone call. My father, the only real parent I had ever known, had left this earth, at the age of eight-two, to be with his Heavenly Father, in whom he trusted for forgiveness and salvation. My father wasn't perfect, he would be the first to tell you that, but he lived what he believed, even if it meant that in the end, he would be expelled from nearly every mainstream Amish church.

It was a large funeral, over one thousand people were in attendance, and the family sat in the main house for the services. However, all the attendees that were from churches that had expelled dad had their own services in a nearby shed. After the service was over, we filed out, one by one, past the Coffin, and said a silent goodbye. This was heart wrenching for me. Somehow, I was able to compose myself at the graveyard, where dad was the first and only one to ever be buried there.

After several years had passed, I found a large stone in the barn foundation, on the original farm where I was born. I painstakingly inscribed all of Dad's information on it, then Denise and I, along with Dave Lee, my brother-in-law, set it at his grave for a headstone. Every few years, I visit his grave and erect a new bird house nearby. Dad remains alone, in death, as he was alone in his conviction against the sin of bed courtship. May the so-called Amish churches who chose sin over righteousness find forgiveness from the Almighty.

It was a clear, sunny, September day. I was driving throughout my area of responsibility, visiting with land owners who had signed up in the Game Commission's Farm Game Program, a program where they agreed to open their land to hunting in exchange for liability insurance on their land. The previous year, I had been assigned to a new position as the Farm, Game Manager. I had 710 signees in my area, and it was my responsibility to visit each one of them at least once a year in case there were any changes to land ownership or their acreage may have changed. I loved my new assignment. I was assigned a pickup truck, and I mostly worked by myself. I got to drive all over a three County area, visiting with folks who seemed genuinely happy to see a representative from the Game Commission at least most of the time.

I was on my way to see the first contact of the day, when, over the radio came an announcement that an airplane had crashed into one of the towers at the World Trade Center in N.Y. City. I was shocked. I couldn't understand how a plane could just crash into something, that big. A little later, Denise called me on my flip phone and asked if I had heard the news. I told her I had heard it on the radio. She told me that she was watching it on TV at her parents' house. I wasn't far from there, so I drove to their house to see what was going on.

When I saw it on TV, I couldn't believe what was happening. It was a terrible sight, one that will remain seared in my memory forever. A few minutes later, right in front of our eyes, another plane flew into the other tower. I was beginning to think, *this can't be just an accident; surely, someone is trying to do us harm.* Sure enough, they began reporting that a plane had flown into the Pentagon, and another one was still missing. Later, they reported that the missing plane had crashed into a field near Shanksville, Pa.

After watching both towers collapse and still reeling with emotions, I left in my truck to inform the other two employees of what was happening. I knew where they were working that day, and that they didn't have cell phone coverage, so, after driving out to the Game lands where they were, I told them that we might be under some type of attack. After they turned their radio on to listen, I left and continued to work the rest of the day.

During the rest of that fateful day and the days following, I felt the urge to go back into the military. It was almost thirteen years since I had walked away from the Coast Guard. I was now thirty-eight years old and dead nuts in the middle of a good career that I wasn't willing to give up.

I began to think about the Army National Guard. I wasn't keen about the Army, because of all the running they required from their soldiers. I had heard of the Air National Guard but didn't know if there were any bases nearby. I heard on the news, that the military recruiters were being swamped with prior service people requesting to re-enlist. I knew exactly why they wanted to go back in. I was feeling the same way. It was time to help kick someone's ass for attacking us. I wanted, in some way, to be a part of it. I was aware that one of the Game Wardens had retired from the National Guard, but I didn't know from which one, so, I decided to contact him.

When I saw him a few days later, he told me that he had retired from the Air National Guard, located in Middletown, Pa., only thirty-five miles from where I lived. Imagine that! He offered to give me a contact number for a recruiter so I could at least talk to him and see what it was all about.

Later that evening, I decided to ask Denise how she would feel about me joining the National Guard, not knowing what to expect. I was a little surprised when she said that she would support my decision. Either way, a few days later I made the call. When I told the recruiter how old I was, I sort of expected him to start laughing, then hang up the phone, but he did no such thing. He said, "Okay, you have four years active duty, the requirement is, you must be able to achieve twenty years of service before you turn sixty years old, so, you are now thirty-eight and you need sixteen more years, so, that would make you fifty-four years old." I was thrilled he said that I would keep my E-4 paygrade, but I would have to take a physical and the ASVAB again. In the meantime, he would start a background investigation.

I was apprehensive. After all, I had been out of the service going on thirteen years. I wondered if I would still be able to meet all the requirements necessary. I didn't have long to wait. Soon I had an appointment for my physical. I passed with no issues. Next, the ASVAB. 2 ½ hours later I was finished, things were moving fast. The recruiter called me to inform me that my ASVAB score was high enough that I could have any job I wanted in aircraft maintenance. Then he gave me an appointment to come in to see him.

The National Guard would require me to serve one weekend per month and fifteen days per year as a minimum, however if they needed me for additional duty, they would simply issue orders for me to report. As far as the state was concerned, as long as I had orders from my unit, they didn't care how long I was away from my job with the Game Commission, so it was a win for me either way. Soon I would meet the recruiter.

CHAPTER
21

To Serve With Honor

Almost two weeks passed before the recruiter called me again. This time he informed me that my background investigation was finished, and he asked me to come in to see him so we could go over some of the paperwork. When I arrived at his office, he asked some questions, and I signed a bunch of papers. After that, he took me on a tour of the maintenance department to see what shop may have an opening for me.

I was a little disappointed when I learned that the structural shop was fully manned already. I had my heart set on that shop. I thought it would be interesting to make structural repairs on the aircraft. Turns out that the only shop with an opening, at least at the moment, was the NDI shop. This shop performed Non-Destructive Inspections on the airplanes. They inspected the air frames for structural failures, such as corrosion, stress cracks, anything abnormal that would compromise the structural integrity of the airframe. There were five methods used to find these malfunctions: Ex-ray, Magnetic Particles, Dye Penetrant, Ultrasound, and Eddy Currant. I thought it sounded interesting. I had never done anything quite like it, so I told the recruiter to sign me up. He told me that I would have to attend a ten-week school at the Navel Air Station in Pensacola, Florida. I sure didn't mind that. I was thinking, *this will be fun.*

When Denise and I had talked about me signing up, I told her that my intentions were to finish my twenty years, then retire. She agreed that that sounded like a plan. The next time I went to see the recruiter, it was to enlist. Denise went along to the base to witness my enlistment. It was a beautiful spring day in 2002 when we arrived at the base, then met with the recruiter. He took us to the Administration building, where we were met by a female officer who was assigned to administer the oath. Then, once again, seventeen years after my first enlistment, I raised my right hand and swore to defend and serve my country with honor. Shortly after that we were issued our Military ID cards. I was handed my orders to report the following weekend for my first Guard Drill; my uniforms would be issued at that time.

As I drove to the base the morning of my first drill weekend, I was a little apprehensive, not because I felt out of place or too old. I was afraid I might've forgotten some of the Military's customs and courtesies, and I didn't want to look like a Jack wagon in front of everyone. Then, as I entered through the gate, I felt reasonably calm. I knew these were my brothers and sisters, after all. I couldn't help but think how far I had come since leaving the Amish so many years ago. I was no longer shy about telling people where I came from. In fact I was rather proud of my upbringing. I was very proud to be a part of the Armed Forces again. I was doggedly determined to serve my country to the best of my ability.

I must say, that first weekend flew by, It seemed there was an endless amount of paperwork to fill out, I had to get my uniforms, attend maintenance meetings with the other maintenance personnel, and there was training to schedule. That weekend, I applied for my school in Florida. My school date wouldn't be until the following October. The Monday following my first drill, I went back to my job with the Game Commission. I was certain I had made a good choice enlisting again. It was fun to do something so different, if only for one weekend a month.

After enlistment, 2002

Previously, when I served in the Coast Guard, it was regulated by the Department of Transportation, while the other four services—Army, Navy, Airforce, and Marines—all fell under the Department of Defense, although they all had, basically, the same benefits and veteran status. The Coast Guard continued to serve under the DOT until after 9-11, when then President George W. Bush placed them under a new department called Homeland Security.

Now that I had enlisted in the Air National Guard, I found myself serving under the Department of Defense. The Air Force had few old-time, traditions. Most of their traditions had started after WWII. The Airforce, during WWII, was called the Army Air corps. It wasn't until 1947 that the Air Force was officially established as a new branch of the service. Of course they began to adopt their own customs and traditions, which to me, weren't nearly as interesting as those of the older branches, but this being one of my only options, I was determined to make the most of it.

October finally arrived. I was getting ready to drive to Pensacola, Florida for ten weeks, while I attended NDI school. This would be the first time Denise and I were separated for more than just a few days, and neither one of us knew quite what to expect. I hated to leave her for that long. She was working full time, and now she would be responsible for everything while I was gone. She told me not to worry, that if she needed anything at all, her family would be able to help her. She wanted me to concentrate on graduating.

A few days later, my orders in hand, I left for Florida. I had decided to drive, since I had no intentions of being stuck for ten weeks without any wheels. In preparation, I had packed my metal detector, along with a couple of fishing poles, with plans to fish in the ocean on weekends and evenings to help pass the time. That evening, I stopped at a motel approximately twenty miles outside of the Naval base for the night. Check-in at the school wasn't until the next day, and I wanted a night just to relax.

The following day, I drove to the base and checked into my room. Because I was prior service, I was given my own room. However, I shared a bathroom with another prior service guy. Overall, it was relatively quiet, basically just a bedroom with a small attached kitchen with a microwave and a small refrigerator, everything I would need to survive.

My school was located on the second floor of what was called the mega building, located within walking distance of my room. Every day I would get a lunch break, where I would return to my room and relax for a few minutes. Then after classes were over in the afternoon, I would walk to the Chow-hall for supper, not every time, sometimes, it was easier to go to the Commissary and get a hoagy. I wasn't crazy about standing in line at the chow hall.

There were around nine students in my class, three of us were prior service. There was another E-4 like me, however he was much younger and had just recently separated from the Air Force, after which, he joined the

Oklahoma National Guard. The other student was a member of the Jordanian Air Force, a foreign student sent here to learn our methods of NDI. I never quite knew what his official rank was. Heck, he could barely speak English. All the rest were newbies, fresh out of boot camp, we paid them very little mind, actually, other than interacting during classes, we weren't supposed to fraternize with them in any way. The three of us were okay with that. The first morning of the class, we introduced ourselves and announced what unit we were from. After that we were given the rules and expectations. Shortly after that, the instructor looked at me and said, "Senior Airman, Troyer, you are the class leader."

I said, "Yes Sir."

He then told me that I was responsible for the cleanliness of the classroom, each night, also if any student had a problem with anything, they were to come to me first. If it was something that I didn't have the resources to handle, I would then be obliged to present their concern to the proper individuals. I wasn't crazy about the added responsibilities; I wanted to be able to concentrate fully on my studies without worrying about all this other crap, but then I remembered why I enlisted in the first place, to serve with honor.

You might be wondering why I was chosen as class leader instead of the other E-4. Well, when there are two individuals of the same rank, then, the one that was promoted first is considered senior. Since I was promoted in 1987, I had about thirteen years of seniority on him.

The Monday of every week there would be a timed test, called a block test. This test would cover everything that we were taught during the previous week. After a few weeks, it became evident that the three of us prior service guys were scoring much higher than the newbies, and the difference between our scores were generally only a point or so apart. It didn't take long until we started competing with one another. What surprised me and the other E-4, was that we couldn't pull away from the Jordanian student, and to my frustration, I could never quite catch him. We couldn't figure him out. His English wasn't any better than when he started. How in the world was he doing it?

Some time, during those ten weeks, I contracted an awful sickness. I still refer to it as a-Southern swamp disease—I had a fever every day, for an entire week, with constant, deep chest coughing, and sleepless nights. I never missed a single class, nor did I dare go to sick call, for fear they would order bed rest. I couldn't afford to lose a single point on my overall score. It wasn't long until the Jordanian came down with the same disease. He actually passed out in class one day, and he also refused to miss a class or go to sick call. Eventually I took pity on him and took some food and medicine to his room one evening. In the meantime, the Oklahoman kept his beady eyes on us, probably hoping we would be forced to remain in bed at least one day, so he would have a better chance of maintaining his score lead. We did not wish him well, but for some reason he never caught our illness.

Sometime after my illness, Denise flew to Pensacola for a weekend to visit me. I still had a lingering cough but was feeling good otherwise. I would study a while in the morning and in the evenings, the rest of the time we spent exploring the pan handle of Florida. We even slipped over to Alabama and spent a night in Louisiana. The second time she flew down to visit was over Thanksgiving, and since we had nowhere in particular to go, we went to the Porch Creek Indian Reservation, where they were serving a Thanksgiving lunch for a fee. I believe it was 7.00 for a paper plate with Turkey and all the fixings. It remains, to this day, the most memorable Thanksgiving dinner we've ever had.

The Pensacola Naval Air Station also held a US Marine detachment, a highly motivated, well-disciplined, hard-drinking, getting-up-early bunch of guys and girls. Every morning, well before my alarm was set to go off, I would be awakened by a formation of Marines running past our barracks, singing cadence at the top of their lungs. I know why they did it. It was a matter of pride, a way to show the other services that the Marines were up and at it while everyone else was still snoozing in bed. It never bothered me. I respected the Marines too much for that.

Personally, I never wanted to be a Marine, mostly because I didn't enjoy running all that much, especially at 0-dark-thirty in the morning, but I always admired them for their toughness and discipline. One morning while walking to the Mega-building for school, I heard a commotion ahead of me on the sidewalk. When I looked up, I saw two Marine Gunnery Sergeants screaming into the face of a newbie Marine, and, from what I gathered, the major offence committed by the newbie was, he had failed to tuck his pants into his boots perfectly, and no one was going to disrespect the Marine uniform in such a way. When I was about even with them, I heard one of them scream, "Now bend over and unf**k your s**t."

I smiled as I strolled by, thinking to myself, *way to go*. If I were to say that to one of the Air Force newbies, they would likely find a corner to cry in, or ask to see a psychiatrist, and I would be sent away to many weeks of sensitivity training. That is exactly why I respected the Marine Corp, they could take a beating verbally, correct their actions, then move on.

We had finally reached the end of our ten-week school, we had taken our last test, now the instructor would compile our score average for the entire ten weeks. The next day, during graduation, anyone with an average above a 95% would be recognized by the instructors, and a certificate would be forwarded to our units. To my displeasure, one of our tests fell during my awful sickness, and halfway through taking it, I had suffered a mental block, forcing me to wing several of the answers in order to finish in my allotted time. Until then, I had a chance to move ahead of at least one of my competitors, but because of my mental block, I was sure I would come in dead last. Now my biggest concern was that the Jordanian might have a chance to finish first. We couldn't allow that to happen. It was simply a matter of pride.

During the ceremony, three of us were called to the front. Only the three prior service guys were able to maintain an above 95% average and were awarded certificates. I held a 97% average, the Jordanian a 98%, and the Oklahoman was the winner with a 99%, average. The highest average held by the newbies was an 87%. I was just happy to be going home at last. I can't say that I wasn't a little proud of that young Amish kid, though, with only an 8th grade education. Turns out, my unit was proud of me as well, and they proved it by awarding me with the Pa. Achievement Metal.

I can't say that I wasn't a little sad about leaving the warmer climate of Florida and returning to the mid-winter weather of Pa. I really liked that part of Florida. It was nice to be able to go fishing, even in the winter, wearing a long-sleeved shirt.

Pa. was going to feel extra cold when I returned, and I wasn't looking forward to that. I was, however, looking forward to being home with Denise. I knew that I would be given orders to report to my Unit for thirty days as soon as I returned, primarily for training purposes. It was designed as a time when everything was still fresh from the school to actually use what I had learned on the job, and hopefully instill it in my brain before I had time to dump it. After I returned home, Denise and I enjoyed the weekend together, then the following Monday, I reported to the base for duty and the start of a wonderful career.

CHAPTER

22

The Air National Guard

There were basically two types of people that were assigned to my unit. One group was called technicians; they were full time people, one or two, sometimes more, in every shop. They were Unionized and considered State Employees. Then there were the Guardsmen, guys like me, who had full time jobs on the outside, but would put on our uniforms one weekend a month and fifteen days per year, minimum. We could be given additional orders at any time, if we were needed. The 193rd was the most deployed Air National Guard unit in the State. The reason for maintaining a bunch of Guardsmen or weekend Warriors, as they are commonly called, is to have a ready reserve of mostly trained warriors ready to be activated, and with a small amount of additional training they would be ready to join the fight. During the Afghan and Iraq wars, Guardsmen from across the Nation made up a large portion of the troops that were deployed into harm's way.

In the military's version of NDI, there are three levels of qualifications: 3, 5 and 7. Graduating from school made you a three level. As a three level, you could do inspections, but only under direct supervision of a five or seven level. As you progressed with your on the job training and got proficient with one of your five methods, you could be advanced to a five level, but only in that method, and so on you would progress until you were signed off on all five methods. Normally it takes at least a year to achieve five level status on all five methods. Then to get upgraded to seven level, we were required to attend a two-week seven level school in Pensacola, Florida.

March 2003, shortly after completing the required thirty-day training period following my school, the US. Invaded Iraq. Immediately, most National Guard Units were activated, including the 193rd, so during my first year, I was activated for ninety days, and because of the additional opportunities to train, I was able to earn my five level status, in less than a year. This was followed by a promotion to Staff Sergeant, the Air Force version of an NCO. Now I was able to perform inspections by myself with minimal supervision.

Our base had a number of C-130 cargo planes. They were old, built in the 1960s, I believe. These planes were being deployed to Iraq for a period of time, then returned for inspections, only to return back to what we referred to as The sand box. A returning plane needed a lot of work and a lot of inspections. During that time, I was at the top of my game as an inspector. I truly enjoyed being busy. Some days it would be ninety degrees out on the flight line, where I would be hunkered down inside a center wing compartment, inspecting the wing structure. It was almost unbearable at times. Evenings, while driving home, I would think of how lucky I was to be able to help in the war effort. I was proud to be able to serve my country.

Approximately a year after becoming a five level, I returned to Pensacola to attend my two- week seven level school. Soon after I graduated, I was raised to seven level status. Now I was considered a top level inspector.

Prior to my seven level school, I had attended a leadership seminar and a train the trainer course, and because of that, I was now a certified trainer, so I was tasked with training the new troops in our shop as well as performing my share of inspections. Since I had joined the NDI shop it had gone through a complete personnel turnover. I was the only original person left. There were now two full time Technical Sergeants who ran the shop, and one of them wasn't fully trained yet, so I assisted in training him.

In the meantime I had completed all my volumes and tasks for E-6, Tech. Sergeant. In the Guard units, there were only a certain amount of positions assigned to each shop, so, even though I had met all the requirements for a promotion, I had to wait for a position to open. After that, if the superintendent recommended me for a promotion, I would still have to endure sitting in front of a panel of Sergeants as they took turns grilling me with questions. Only after earning their approval, would I be promoted. As luck would have it, one of the full time Tech. Sergeants decided to get a job in another state, so I was promoted to Technical Sergeant to fill his position. A short while after being promoted to Tech. Sergeant, I was once again summoned to sit before another oral board. This time I was competing against others for the Tech. Sergeant of the quarter award. After the results were analyzed by the decision makers, I felt very honored to be chosen as the winner.

Working two careers simultaneously certainly had its challenges at times. With so many different things going on in my life, it was a challenge focusing on the job at hand. I seemed to be doing very well in both jobs though, as I had recently been promoted to a crew Supervisors position with the Game Commission. Now I had to focus on work results with the Game commission as well as manage my training requirements with the ANG. Weirdly, I found that the more responsibilities that were placed on me, the more I wanted. I had a strong desire to accomplish as much as possible in my life. Some folks tried to convince me that I needed to slow down, while others encouraged me to press on. I really didn't need any encouragement though. I intended to live my life at its fullest, and so I pressed on.

Sometime after becoming a Tech. Sergeant, the shop chief was taken ill, and had to retire on disability. Suddenly, not only was I the highest ranking person in our shop, but I was also the only qualified NDI inspector. The maintenance superintendent suddenly found himself in a quandary. He didn't have any inspectors, except me, and I was a part time Guardsman. He confronted me and asked if I might have a solution to his problem. I told him that if he would call me at my Game Commission job, whenever he had inspections that he needed to get done, I would drive the forty minutes to the base after work and do the required inspections until he could find a replacement. So, for the next four months, that is what I did several times a week. After the replacements were hired and had returned from NDI school, I was tasked with training four individuals simultaneously, two full time, and two Guardsmen, until one of them had achieved a five level. For this I was awarded the Air Force Achievement Metal. Whether I deserved it or not, I felt honored.

In spite of everything that was going on, I somehow, found time to study the required courses for Master Sergeant, not that I expected to be promoted to that rank as a Guardsmen, but I figured I would be ready, just in case. I also attended evening classes at the Community College until I earned an Associate's Degree in Applied Science. This wasn't a requirement for either career, but rather a personal milestone I wanted to reach.

I guess it was a good thing, taking out the Master Sergeants course, because six years before I planned to retire, the shop chief suddenly took ill and was forced to retire. Guess who was standing in the wings, with all his requirements completed for Master Sergeant? You guessed it. After being recommended for the position by the Superintendent, I sat through another grueling oral board, then soon after that, I was promoted to the paygrade of Master Sergeant. I felt I had reached a pinnacle in my life somehow. Certainly, not all by myself, but with the help and guidance of others.

Filling the role as shop chief was a whole new ballgame. Now, I found myself immersed in policy enforcement, along with personnel issues that had to be resolved. I didn't hate it at all, but I did miss the days when I only had to be concerned with inspections. Regrettably, I found that I had less and less time to actually do inspections.

Six years as a Master Sergeant passed by quicker than I expected. Before I realized what was happening, it was 2017. It was hard to believe that I had now served my country a full twenty years. I was now fifty-four years old, and I felt as if I had fulfilled my obligation to my homeland. With a satisfied mind, I began to make preparations to retire from the Air National Guard. I had been treated well, and I would miss it, especially my brothers and sisters in arms. So, I picked a day in June to say my final goodbyes. There would be a ceremony, and I would be expected to say something, a speech of sorts. I decided not to write anything down, but rather speak from the heart.

The day of retirement had arrived. My wife went along to the base to help in my celebration. It wasn't lost on me that without Denise quietly picking up the slack, in the background, my career may not have been possible. I want to thank all the unsung heroes, serving those who serve.

My ceremony started at 11:30. There were around thirty enlisted and seven or eight officers present, including the Base Commander. I was presented with several certificates, flags that had been flown over the State Capital and the base, congratulation letters from a State Senator and a Congressman, several of my friends made comments, wishing me well. Then the Commander called everyone to attention, and the order was read for me to receive the Air Force, Meritorious Service Metal, a decoration I did not expect, nor was I sure I had earned. Then it was my turn to speak from the heart. The following is what I said.

U. S. Air force, Retirement speech 6-10-17, 193rd S.O.W.

Well then, here we are!

I sure don't feel worthy of this crowd.

First, I want to thank God and my wife, in that order. Denise has put up with me for twenty-six years, and she was the rock I leaned on throughout my career, so thank you. (I went on to thank the Col., Lt. Col. And other ranking officials for their leadership and support.)

As some of you already know. I come from humble beginnings, as a young boy growing up Amish in the late 60s and early 70s, I always dreamed of being in law enforcement, or the military, and even though at times that dream seemed impossible to achieve, I never gave up.

In 1985 at the age of twenty-two, I left the Amish to pursue my dream but found that I was missing three things.

I didn't have a birth certificate, a driver's license, or a G.E.D. fortunately, within three months I was able to acquire all three, and on April 22, 1985, I entered boot camp for the United States Coast Guard, one of the proudest moments of my life.

Since than I have had the honor and privilege, of serving with some of the greatest individuals I have ever met in my life, and that is all of you.

I have never looked at my service as a duty, but rather as a privilege, and I want to thank all of you for allowing me to serve alongside of you, in the greatest Military, in the greatest, absolutely the greatest nation on earth. Again, thanks to all of you. And thank you all for coming. That is all I have.

After the ceremony had ended, I returned to the shop, where I had spent the last sixteen years. I took some time to reflect over my military career, and I was satisfied.

I continued to work for the Pa. Game Commission for another three years. Then after thirty years of dedicated service to the agency, I decided that it was time to retire from there. I felt I had done much for wildlife and the Sportsmen of Pa. There wasn't much more I could do here. Besides, I had a few more things I wanted to accomplish yet in life, this book being one of them.

EPILOGUE

Almost four decades have passed since I departed from the sanctity of my Old Order Amish church, the place I would be remanded to for life had others had their wish. My leaving, against all odds, is a testament to man's desire to live free, and in some cases, as was mine, at a great personal cost.

In 2010, Denise and I were able to purchase what was left of the old homestead where I was born. The house was beyond repair, so after tearing it down, we constructed a new house, and in 2013, I completed my circle when we moved into our new house within mere feet of where I grew up.

A few years later, we were able to purchase thirty acres in northwest Montana, where we built a second home, where we spend as much time as possible. Who knows, someday we may leave these old memories and move out there. For me, life goes on, and until my journey ends on this earth, I shall continue to live.

When I left the Amish, I didn't really know what to believe, concerning God. I believed there was a God, but just didn't worry much about it. I had come to doubt almost everything the Amish tried to tell me, including that I was headed for Hell in a hand basket, because of my wicked ways. I, however, never forgot about the Lord, and many years later, I got down on my knees, confessed my sins, and accepted Jesus as my Savior. I certainly don't live a perfect life, and I need forgiveness always, but my Savior knows my heart, and I know he loves me. For that I am humbly grateful.

I am not ashamed of my Amish roots. In fact, quite the opposite is true. It is because of my upbringing, the hardships and turmoil, the work ethics that I was taught, all of these things combined, that made me who I am today. Of course, the dishonesty, and back-biting of some also made me abhor those particular traits, and so, I tried to avoid making those same mistakes.

I can only hope, as I stumbled and fought my way through this life, that I may have been a good example to others. Maybe I gave someone hope when there wasn't any, or even proved that odds, which seem insurmountable can, with sheer will, be overcome. I certainly was helped by kind people throughout my journey, and I have tried to help others whenever I could.

I tried to refrain from using any offensive language throughout this book, but in the process of telling my story with real meaning, I may have nudged up against the wire a few times. If anyone is offended, I apologize. Please take a moment and black out the few words that you may find offensive. I hope you find this book to be inspirational and interesting, Thank you for taking the time to read it.